Horse Symbolism
The Horse in Mythology, Religion, Folklore, and Art

By: Gloria Austin and Mary Chris Foxworthy
President of:
Equine Heritage Institute, Inc. (EHI)

First Publish Date 2019

Gloria Austin Carriage Collection, LLC; Equine Heritage Institute, Inc.
3024 Marion County Road Weirsdale, FL 32195 Office: (352) 753-2826 Fax: (352) 753-6186

Ordering Information:
Quantity sales: Special discounts are available on quantity purchases by corporations, associations, and others. For details, contact the publisher at the address above.
Printed in the United States of America First Edition ISBN 978-1-7320805-8-4

Our Mission Statement: *To educate, celebrate, and preserve the history of the horse and its role in shaping world civilizations and changing lives.*

www.equineheritageinstitute.org
www.equineheritagemuseum.com

EQUINE HERITAGE INSTITUTE

Please contact:
Gloria Austin
3024 Marion County Road
Weirsdale, FL 32195
Phone: 352-753-2826
Fax: 352-753-6186
www.gloriaaustin.com

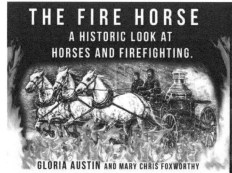

THE FIRE HORSE
A HISTORIC LOOK AT HORSES AND FIREFIGHTING.

GLORIA AUSTIN AND MARY CHRIS FOXWORTHY

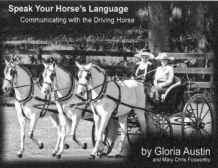

Speak Your Horse's Language
Communicating with the Driving Horse

by Gloria Austin
and Mary Chris Foxworthy

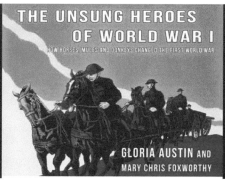

THE UNSUNG HEROES OF WORLD WAR I
HOW HORSES, MULES AND DONKEYS CHANGED THE FIRST WORLD WAR

GLORIA AUSTIN AND MARY CHRIS FOXWORTHY

The Golden Carriage and The House of Hapsburg

by Gloria Austin

The Gloria Austin Carriage Collection

Updated Edition

by Gloria Austin, Linda Beaulieu and Jeffrey Batchelder

From a European Full State Carriage to American Road Carts
A Comprehensive Collection

Carriage Lamps

Why Not Own EHI's Entire Library of Equine Knowledge?
https://amzn.to/2NsUoeX

EQUINE HERITAGE INSTITUTE

Horses of the Americas

From the Prehistoric Horse, to Modern American Breeds.

The BREWSTER STORY

AMERICA'S PREMIER CARRIAGE BUILDERS AND HISTORICAL EVENTS LEADING TO, DURING, AND AFTER THE BREWSTER ERA.
By Gloria Austin & Linda Beaulieu

A Thank You Gift of
EQUINE ELEGANCE

By Gloria Austin

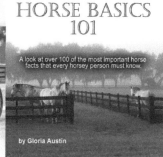

HORSE BASICS 101

A look at over 100 of the most important horse facts that every horsey person must know.

by Gloria Austin

A Drive Through Time: Carriages, Horses and History

EQUINE HERITAGE INSTITUTE

BY GLORIA AUSTIN, STEPHANIE SUTCH AND LINDA BEAULIEU

The Horse, History and Human Culture

by Gloria Austin

A Review of the horse's impact on man's culture, society and life.

A Glossary Of Harness Parts And Related Terms

by Gloria Austin

The Horse

"We have had 6,000 years of history with the domesticated horse and only 100 years with the automobile."

Gloria Austin

The Automobile

| 4000 BC | 3000 BC | 2000 BC | 1000 BC | 0 | 1000 AD | PRESENT |

TABLE OF CONTENTS

INTRODUCTION

Why is it that so many children wish they had a horse?

There was a time when horses were a necessity; not something of wishful dreams. Once the horse was replaced by the car, it did not take long for the movie industry and television to romanticize horses. Horse heroes were everywhere! But even before the horse was supplanted by motorized vehicles and airplanes, horses filled the hearts and imaginations of societies and artists and authors. Horses were important in mythology, religion, and legends and played a crucial role in the history of civilization!

It's those myths and legends that fill a child's imagination with their own ideas of slaying a dragon with the help of a magnificent steed or riding through an enchanted forest on a horse with a flowing mane and tail. We hope you enjoy the myths, legends, and stories in this book. Some tales you may even share with a horse crazy child. In the process, you might decide that, if you don't already own a horse, you may NEED a horse! So, at this end of the book, we give you some helpful tips for finding your very own "unicorn."

The Unicorn

The unicorn is the only fabulous beast that does not seem to have been conceived out of human fears. In even the earliest references he is fierce yet good, selfless yet solitary, but always mysteriously beautiful. Those who drank from its horn were thought to be protected from stomach trouble, epilepsy, and poison. It was very fleet of foot and difficult to capture.

The oldest description of a unicorn occurs in the Epic of Gilgamesh, an epic poem from ancient Mesopotamia. The first surviving version of the poem dates to the 18th century BC and recounts the deeds of Gilgamesh, the king of Uruk. Unicorns are referred to in the ancient myths of India and China as well. One suggestion is that the unicorn is based on the extinct animal Elasmotherium, a huge Eurasian rhinoceros native to the steppes. The 13th-century traveler, Marco Polo, claimed to have seen a unicorn in Java, but his description makes it clear to the modern reader that he saw a Java Rhinoceros.

Greek writers on natural history were convinced of the reality of the unicorn, so unicorns do not appear in Greek mythology. The earliest description in Greek literature of a single-horned animal was by the historian Ctesias (c. 400 BCE). Ctesias related that the Indian wild ass was the size of a horse, with a white body, purple head, blue eyes, and on its forehead was a cubit-long horn colored red at the pointed tip, black in the middle, and white at the base.

As a biblical animal, the unicorn was interpreted allegorically in the early Christian church. One of the earliest such interpretations appears in the ancient Greek bestiary known as the Physiologus, which states that the unicorn is a strong, fierce animal that can be caught only if a virgin maiden is thrown before it. The unicorn then would leap into the virgin's lap, and she would lead it to the king's palace. Medieval writers thus likened the unicorn to Christ, who raised up a horn of salvation for mankind and dwelt in the womb of the Virgin Mary. *(cited from: https://www.britannica.com/topic/unicorn and http://www.sheppardsoftwarecom/Europeweb/factfile/Unique-facts-Europe30.htm)* The unicorn has been used in heraldry for a very long time. *(below)*

A long time ago, when the earth was still green,
There were more kinds of animals than you've ever seen;
They'd run around free while the earth was being born,
The loveliest of all was the Unicorn.

There were green alligators and long-necked geese,
Some humpty-backed camels and some chimpanzees,
Some cats and rats and elephants, but sure as you're born,
The loveliest of all was the Unicorn.

Now God seen some sinnin' and it gave Him pain.
And He said, "Stand back, I'm going to make it rain."
He said, "Hey, brother Noah, I'll tell you what to do.
Build me a floating zoo."

And take some of them green alligators and long-necked geese,
Some humpty-backed camels, and some chimpanzees,
Some cats and rats and elephants, but sure as you're born,
Don't you forget my Unicorn."

Old Noah was there to answer the call,
He finished up making the Ark just as the rain started fallin',
He marched in the animals two by two
And he called out as they went through,
"Hey, Lord: I've got yer...

Green alligators and long-necked geese,
Some humpty-backed camels and some chimpanzees,
Some cats and rats and elephants, but Lord, I'm so forlorn,
I just can't see no Unicorn."

Old Noah looked out into the driving rain,
Them Unicorns was hiding, playing silly games,
Kicking and splashing while the rain was pouring,
Oh, them silly Unicorns.

There was green alligators and long-necked geese,
Some humpty-backed camels and some chimpanzees,
Noah cried, "Close the doors 'cause the rain is pourin',
And we just can't wait for no Unicorns."

The Ark started movin', it drifted with the tide,
Them Unicorns looked up from the rock and they cried,
And the waters came down and sorta' floated them away,
That's why you'll never see a Unicorn, to this very day.

You'll see green alligators and long-necked geese,
Some humpty-backed camels and some chimpanzees,
Some cats and rats and elephants, but sure as you're born,
You're never gonna see no Unicorn.

(cited from: Silverstein, Shel. Where The Sidewalk Ends : the Poems & Drawings of Shel Silverstein. New York :HarperCollins, 2004.)

Horses in Mythology

Every culture has some type of mythology. Most people are familiar with the classical mythology of the ancient Greeks and Romans. The same types of stories, and often the very same story, can be found in myths from different parts of the world. To the ancients, the meaning of the story was more important than the literal truth or details of the story.

Myths tell the stories of ancestors and the origin of humans, the world, the gods, supernatural beings and heroes with super-human powers. Think of mythology like the comic books of today! Myths also describe origins of long-held customs or explain natural events such as the sunrise and sunset, the full moon or thunder and lightning storms.

Pegasus

Perseus was one of the greatest Greek heroes and slayer of monsters. Medusa was a winged monster with venomous snakes in place of her hair. Anyone who gazed at her turned to stone. Perseus guided himself to her with the reflection of her in his shield and beheaded her as she slept. Pegasus sprang out of Medusa's body when she was beheaded. Following the death of Medusa, Perseus was traveling home on Pegasus when he caught sight of a maiden chained to a rock. The maiden was Andromeda, the daughter of the King and Queen of Ethiopia. Andromeda's mother had angered Poseidon by boasting that her daughter was more beautiful than even the Nereids (the sea nymph goddesses of the sea). Poseidon punished the people of Ethiopia by first sending a flood, and then a sea monster to terrorize them. The only way to appease Poseidon was to sacrifice Andromeda by chaining her to a rock for the sea monster.

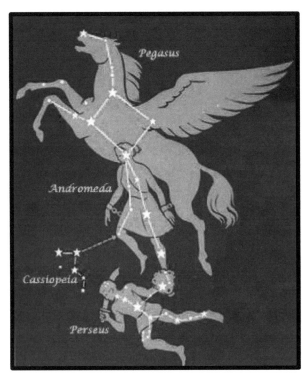

Perseus offered to rescue the princess, and deal with the monster, provided that he be given Andromeda's hand in marriage. The king agreed to this, and when the monster came to claim the princess, it was turned to stone by Perseus with the severed head of Medusa. The connection between Perseus, Pegasus, and Andromeda may be seen in the sky, where their constellations can be found side by side. *(left)*

Pegasus was also the mount of Bellerophon, who came to possess the flying horse during his quest against the chimera - a fire-breathing female monster with a lion's head, a goat's body, and a serpent's tail. Bellerophon visited the city of Tiryns, where Proetus was king. The queen, Stheneboea, fell in love with Bellerophon, but he rejected her advances. Feeling humiliated, Stheneboea went to her husband and accused the hero of trying to seduce her. The enraged Proetus sent Bellerophon to his father-in-law, Iobates, the King of Lycia, with a letter. In the letter, the king was asked to kill the messenger. Instead of putting Bellerophon to death, however, Iobates decided to send the hero on a quest to kill the chimera, believing that he would not survive the encounter. The goddess Athena brought Pegasus to Bellerophon. With the help of Pegasus, Bellerophon succeeded in slaying the chimera. Over time, Bellerophon's pride grew, and he aspired to scale the heights of Mount Olympus on the back of Pegasus to take his place amongst the immortals. *(right)* Zeus was aware of the hero's ambition and sent a gadfly to sting Pegasus. Bellerophon lost his balance and fell back to earth. Pegasus, however, continued the journey to Mount Olympus, and went on to live in Zeus' palace, and was given the task of carrying the god's thunder and lightning. *(cited from: https://www.ancient-origins.net/myths-legends/pegasus-majestic-white-horse-olympus-006182)*

10

Sleipnir

If you have watched the Avengers movies, you have heard of Odin and Loki. But have you heard of Sleipnir?

Sleipnir is Odin's valiant steed, "the best among horses." He carried Odin, the leader of the Norse gods, on many quests, and he never failed to leave common men awestruck by his strength and speed.

During the early days of Midgard, the gods were approached by a builder who offered to build a fortification for them to keep out invaders. The builder claimed that he could complete this fortress in 3 seasons, but in exchange, he wanted the goddess Freyja and the sun and the moon as payment. After a heated debate, the gods agreed to the deal, but they stipulated that no man could help the builder, and if the fortress were not complete in three seasons, he would receive no payment.

When he heard the gods' conditions, the builder begged to be allowed the help of his stallion, Svaoilfair. Loki convinced the other gods to allow this, and the builder began work. Much to the amazement and chagrin of the gods, they soon found that the builder and his stallion were equal to their task. The stallion hauled enormous rocks to the building site day in and day out, and by the time the project's deadline approached, it was clear the builder would finish his work.

The gods were enraged. They had never intended to pay the builder and had depended on him failing to meet the project's deadline. They took their wrath out on Loki, as it was evident that the builder couldn't have completed his task without the help of his stallion. If Loki didn't find a way to interrupt the builder's progress, the gods swore they would sentence him to a cruel death.

Loki was terrified, but his crafty brain didn't fail him. That same night, he shapeshifted into a beautiful mare and went out to attract the builder's stallion. Sure enough, the stallion tore away from the builder and pursued the mare into the forest. Now, it was the builder's turn to be enraged, and in his fury, he revealed that he was actually one of the banished race of giants, so Odin smashed his skull in with his hammer. Sometime later, Loki gave birth to Sleipnir.

Sleipnir was a large, muscular horse with eight legs instead of four. Sleipnir's coat was as gray as a thundercloud, and his mane and tail were streams of darker grey. He could gallop faster, jump higher, kick harder, and whinny louder than any other horse in Asgard. His strength knew no equal, and his heart knew no fear. In addition to racing over the ground, Odin's mighty steed could also fly through the air and swim through water. None of the elements could slow him down. He was even able to ferry Odin safely in and out of Hel, the realm of the dead. *(cited from: https://mythology.net/norse/norse-creatures/sleipnir/)*

The Sun Chariot and Phaeton

A Sun Chariot was found on Trundholm Mose, south of Højby, in September 1902. *(left)* The find dates back to the old Bronze Age, about 1400 B.C. The Sun Chariot, which is made of bronze, consists of a gold-coated disc of the sun, drawn by a horse, both placed on a small six-wheeled chariot. The Sun Chariot consists of the solar disk, the axle, and four wheels with spokes and supports the idea that the sun was drawn on its eternal journey by a divine horse.

According to Greek Mythology, Phaethon, was the son of the Sun-God Helios and a mortal woman, Clymene. However, he was living only with his mother as his father had a difficult task to perform; he was responsible for driving the horse chariot with the sun from the one side of the Earth to the other during the daytime. One day, a school-mate of Phaethon laughed at his claim that he was the son of a god and said he didn't believe him. In tears, Phaethon went to his mother and demanded proof of his paternity. Clymene assured her son that he was indeed the son of the great god Helios and sent him on his way to the palace of his father to establish his legitimacy.

A delighted and hopeful Phaethon traveled to India, as there was the palace of his father who was supposed to begin every day his course from the east. When he reached the palace of Helios, he was astonished at its magnificence and luxury. His eyes were almost blinded by the dazzle of the light all around him. The palace was supported by massive columns adorned with glittering gold and precious stones, while the ceilings and doors were made with polished ivory and silver. Phaethon looked with awe at the exquisite representation of the earth, the sea, and the sky on the walls of the palace. Amazed with all the luxury, he had faced, Phaethon came into the august presence of his reputed father, Helios, sitting on a diamond-studded throne surrounded by the presences of the Day, the Month, the Year, and the Hour. His other attendants included Spring, bedecked with flowers, Summer, with a garland of spear-like ripened grains, Autumn, with feet reddened with grape juice and Winter, with hoar-frost in his hair. Phaethon told Helios about the humiliation he had to suffer because of the imputation of illegitimacy. He pleaded with Helios to recognize him as his son and establish beyond all doubt the legitimacy of his birth.

Helios was deeply moved and firmly affirmed Phaethon's paternity and legitimacy. In fact, he declared, in the presence of all his attendants, that he will gladly grant his son any favor that he would ask him. Phaethon, happy because great Helios had recognized him as his son, decided to test the limits of his father's love and benevolence. The rash boy asked to be allowed to drive the awesome Chariot of the Sun for one day. Helios was fearful at his son's irrational request. He tried to explain to his son that even the mighty Zeus could not presume to drive the Chariot of the Sun, much less a mere mortal. That onerous task was reserved solely for him, god Helios. Unfortunately, once the gods had promised a favor, they could not withdraw or deny it. Helios used all his persuasive skills to plead the rash Phaethon to withdraw his outrageous demand but to no avail. The boy insisted that Helios kept his promise. The god of the Sun could do nothing else but to give in.

Wanting to drive the awesome Chariot of the Sun was one thing, but to actually do it was not as simple as our naive Phaethon had imagined. A helpless Helios tried to warn his son of the dangers involved in driving the Chariot with its fiery horses which even the great god himself had found difficult to control on many occasions. Helios noticed an expression of power and arrogance on his son's face. He advised Phaethon to steer the Chariot through a middle course and not to go too high or too low. As soon as he took off, Phaethon realized that he had taken on more than he could handle. He found himself utterly powerless to control the fiery horses. When the horses realized the weakness and inexperience of their young charioteer, they began to steer a wild and dangerous course. The Chariot of the Sun was said to have blazed a gash in the skies which supposedly became the Milky Way, a spiral galaxy. Then the uncontrollable Chariot of the Sun began to steer a too low course, hitting the earth and unleashing immense destruction, including the burning of the African continent and turning it into desert, making the Ethiopian people black-skinned, since they were burnt from the fire of the Sun, and even causing considerable damage to the river Nile.

The destruction infuriated the chief of the gods, Zeus, who struck the boy down with his thunderbolt. *(left)* The body of the dead Phaethon fell into the Eridanus River, which was later to be known as the river Po of Italy. The unfortunate Phaethon was deeply mourned by his sisters, the Heliades, who were transformed into poplar trees to stand by the river and protect their brother forever. *(cited from: https://www.greeka.com/greece-myths/phaethon.htm)*

13

Seahorses

Some of the oldest seahorse stories tell of the Greek sea god Poseidon galloping through the oceans on a golden chariot pulled by Hippocampus, a half horse, half fish sea animal. Neptune was the god of freshwater and the sea in Roman religion and also had a chariot drawn by seahorses.

The word hippos in Greek means horse and kampos means sea monster. These mythical creatures are believed to have been created from the crests of sea waves. *(left)* Hippocampus were secretive creatures who lived deep in Poseidon's raging seas, but they were not vicious. They never fed on humans but on plants found at the bottom of the ocean. They were portrayed as extremely loyal, graceful, and agile creatures. Ancient Greek fishermen believed the real seahorses they sometimes found tangled in their nets were the offspring of Poseidon's mighty steeds.

Poseidon was on the side of the Greeks in the Trojan War depicted in the Iliad. He had a grudge against Troy because he and his brother, Apollo, were cheated and disrespected by Laomedon, a Trojan hero whom Zeus once sent them to serve for a year. In Book 13 of the Iliad, Poseidon charges toward Troy in his chariot pulled by seahorses. *(right)*

Kelpies

The kelpie is a Scottish, shape-shifting, water horse often associated with fairies. Unlike the seahorses of Poseidon and Neptune, they are very malicious. You don't want a kelpie! They often appear as a beautiful horse near or in running water and can be identified by the mane that seems to be constantly dripping wet. They will sometimes appear as a beautiful woman dressed in green, bent on luring men to their watery doom.

Nearly every river, stream, or lake in Scotland has a kelpie legend. Even the famous Loch Ness Monster could be a kelpie. Noggle is one such Kelpie often described as a grey Shetland pony from the Shetland Islands

When encountered they are alone and often saddled and bridled and ready to ride. This presents an enticing invitation to a weary traveler. A kelpie is said to have magical powers that someone who captures it can use to their advantage. They have the strength of ten normal horses and endurance far beyond that. Once on its back, the kelpie's sticky magical hide will not allow a person to dismount. Once trapped this way, the kelpie will drag the person into the water and then eat them. This is not the only thing a kelpie can do to defend itself from capture. The Kelpie has a tail that can be smacked on the water with such force that a clap of thunder is emitted. The resulting flood can drag a human into the water, where the kelpie will drag them to their death.

A kelpie has a weak spot – its bridle. Anyone who can get hold of a kelpie's bridle will have command over it and any other kelpie. It is rumored that the MacGregor clan have a kelpie's bridle, passed down through the generations and said to have come from an ancestor who took it from a kelpie near Loch Slochd. *(cited from: https://mythology.net/mythical-creatures/kelpie/)*

Arion

Arion was a divinely bred, very swift horse who could talk. In the myth of Heracles, the demigod took the stallion from Oncus. He then rode on Arion during the war and gifted it to Adrastus afterward. *(below)*

When Oedipus was exiled from the city of Thebes, his sons Eteocles and Polynices ascended to the throne. The two brothers had initially agreed to share the throne, and rule in an alternating fashion. However, when Eteocles' time finished and it was Polynices' turn to rule, Eteocles refused and exiled his brother

Polynices traveled to Argos during his exile. There he met Tydeus of Calydon who was also a fugitive from his native country. They met near the palace of Adrastus. The two soon started fighting each other. Adrastus heard them and separated them. He immediately recognized the two men as the men that had been promised to him by an oracle as the future husbands of two of his daughters. One bore on his shield the figure of a boar, and the other that of a lion and the oracle stated that one of his daughters was to marry a boar and the other a lion. Adrastus, therefore, gave his daughter Deipyle to Tydeus, and his daughter Argeia to Polynices. He then promised to lead each of these princes back to his own country. So off to Thebes, he traveled on his swift horse Arion to help Polynices regain his right to the throne.

Adrastus prepared for war against Thebes even though Amphiaraus, the king of Argos, foretold that all who should engage in it should perish, except Adrastus. During the war of "Seven Against Thebes," Adrastus was joined by six other heroes. Just before Eteocles confronted Polynices, he remembered his father's curse that the two brothers would divide the kingdom by the sword. This war ended as unfortunately as Amphiaraus had predicted, and Adrastus alone was saved by the swiftness of his horse Arion.

Sophocles wrote the continuation of the story in his tragedy Antigone. *(cited from: https://www.greekmythology.com/Myths/Mortals/Adrastus/adrastus.html)*

Hazium

In Islamic tradition, Hazium *(left)* is a luminous, white, winged horse. He was given to the Archangel Gabriel by God because God was pleased with Gabriel. Hazium is the heavenly horse upon which the archangel Gabriel delivered direct communication to the prophet Mohammed.

Hazium was a winged horse that appeared to be made of white fire because he was a manifestation of the presence of God. He was so powerful that the sand that touched his hoof brought a golden calf idol to life. Even though Hazium held a great deal of power, he had a heart of love and a desire to serve out of love.

Tianma

During the reign of Emperor Wudi of the Han Dynasty (206 BC-AD 220), China gained prosperity and might that was without precedent.

Mindful of the constant harassment of his country by the steppe nomads, Wudi sought to solve the issue once and for all by forming an invincible cavalry that could strike with the same lightning speed as had those fierce horsemen. These nomads, known as Xiongnu, had once laid siege to his great-grandfather and founder of the Han Empire.

To do that he needed the warhorse, a breed native to the kingdom of Da Yuan, a Central Asian country in the Ferghana Valley. So around 139 BC, the emperor sent out a convoy, headed by a man named Zhang Qian, on a westward journey that eventually took them to Central Asia. Their two most important tasks: to seek a military alliance with other countries at enmity with the Xiongnu and to look for the reputed heavenly horses. These heavenly horses featured longer and spikier ears that made them look more vigilant. *(above right)* They also had elongated bodies that appeared both athletic and elegant. During an eventful journey that lasted thirteen years, Zhang Qian was captured by the Xiongnu twice. When he arrived back in 126 BC, he was accompanied by just one man – and there were no horses. For the Han people the horses had become a fetish and a cult, as evidenced by their assigned name, "heavenly horses." After that, diplomatic groups were dispatched annually by the Han court to Central Asia to buy horses. According to historical records, the Han government even set up breeding grounds in Gansu, hoping to localize the superior genes of the heavenly horses. *(cited from: https://www.telegraph.co.uk/news/world/china-watch/culture/tianma-chinas-heavenly-horses/)*

Longma

The Longma was a horse-like dragon from Chinese mythology. It had the body of a horse, but the scales and head of a Chinese dragon. Some also had wings. Emperor Mu of the Jin-Dynasty had a wagon that was drawn by eight, winged dragon horses. Since it combines the concepts of the sky (dragon) and the earth (horse), it is seen as an embodiment of both elements. Dragon-horses are born by mares who drank from rivers inhabited by dragons.

Edward H. Schafer (noted Chinese historian) described the horse's "tremendous importance" to the Tang Dynasty rulers for military tactics, diplomatic policy, and aristocratic privilege as follows:

"This patrician animal owed his unique status to more than his usefulness to the lords of the land. He was invested with sanctity by ancient tradition, endowed with prodigious qualities, and visibly stamped with the marks of his divine origin. A revered myth proclaimed him a relative of the dragon, akin to the mysterious powers of water. Indeed, all wonderful horses, such as the steed of the pious Hsüan-Tsang which, in later legend, carried the sacred scriptures from India, were avatars of dragons, and in antiquity, the tallest horse owned by the Chinese were called simply dragons." *(cited from: Schafer, Edward H. 1963. The Golden Peaches of Samarkand, a Study of T'ang Exotics. University of California Press. p.59)*

Mares of Diomedes

The Mares of Diomedes were four horses in Greek mythology that ate humans. They belonged to the giant Diomedes, king of Thrace.

Stealing the Mares of Diomedes was one of the tasks that was given to the demigod hero Heracles by King Eurystheus. Heracles did not know that the horses were wild and maddened because of their diet which consisted of human flesh. They were all kept harnessed to a bronze manger. Heracles managed to corner the horses on a peninsula; he then dug a trench and filled it with water, turning the peninsula into an island. When Diomedes arrived, Heracles killed him and fed him to the horses. By feeding the horses with human flesh, they became calm, and Heracles managed to bring them to King Eurystheus. One version has it that the horses had become permanently calm at that point, and were left to roam the countryside. Another version has it that Eurystheus sent them to Olympus as a sacrifice to Zeus, who refused them and sent wolves and lions to kill them.

Not all myths are about beautiful horses with superpowers – but myths make for great movies for actors who portray superheroes *(above: Dwyane "The Rock" Johnson in the movie "Hercules" with the Mares of Diomedes)*

Xanthus and Balius

During the Trojan War, Xanthus and Balius pulled the chariot of Achilles. These powerful horses had the gifts of speech and prophecy.

Achilles' comrade-in-arms Patroclus cared for the horses. In the Iliad, it is told how, when Patroclus was killed in battle, Xanthus and Balius stood motionless on the field of battle, and wept. Automedon, Achilles' charioteer, *(left with Xanthus and Balius)* stated that only Patroclus was able to fully control these horses. When Xanthus was rebuked by the grieving Achilles for allowing Patroclus to be slain, Hera granted Xanthus human speech which broke divine law, allowing the horse to say that a god had killed Patroclus and that a god would soon kill Achilles too. After this, the Erinyes (also known as the Furies – goddesses of vengeance) struck the horse dumb.

Chollima

The Chollima is a winged horse in Korean mythology that is too swift and elegant to be mounted by a mortal. The Chomilla could gallop 1,100 kilometers in a day; the entire length of the Korean peninsula. The Chollima wanted to be tamed but having found no one able to tame him, he flew up into the sky.

Chollima is, in modern day, a very influential figure in North Korea. State propaganda brought him back to earth and depicted him being tamed by the proletariat. An impressive 46-meter-tall statue of Chollima *(left)* was built in downtown Pyongyang, depicting the winged horse carrying on his back a worker holding a Korean Workers Party address and a woman carrying rice. The Chollima has lent its name to a Pyeongannam-do (South Pyeongan Province) county, as well as the national soccer team, a movie studio, and even North Korea's 1956 answer to China's Great Leap Forward, intended to promote rapid economic development. *(cited from: https://korea.lablob.com/2011/12/18/supernatural-creatures-of-korean-mythology/)*

21

Gullfaxi

Gullfaxi *(left)* was a horse in Norse mythology. Its name means "golden mane." He was the swift horse of the giant Hrungnir.

One day the giant encountered Odin mounted on Sleipnir. Odin said he would wager his head that there was no horse in Jötunheimr that would prove equally to Sleipnir. Hrungnir declared he had a much better horse named Gullfaxi. He vaulted upon Gullfaxi and galloped after Odin, all the way into Ásgarðr. There he challenged Thor to single-combat at the place called Grjótúnagard. Hrungnir was killed in the duel and fell forward upon Thor so that his foot lay over the god's neck. No one was strong enough to lift the foot off Thor until Thor's son Magni came up and easily cast the giant's foot aside. In gratitude, Thor gave Gullfaxi to Magni. This displeased Odin, who said that Thor did wrong to give a good horse to his son and not to his own father. *(cited from: https://pantheon.org/articles/g/gullfaxi.html)*

Caballo

Caballo *(right)* was a sea horse in the mythology of Chile. It was an invisible creature that could only be seen by people with magical powers. The Caballo looked like a horse with a golden mane but had 4 paws in the form of fins and a long tail similar to a fish. Wizards and dead sailors traveled to El Caleuche (a phantom ship) on the back of the Caballo.

Horses in Religion

A study of religious practices reveals that horses had an important part to play in the formation and development of human spirituality. Horses have been worshipped since the Bronze Age. They have been consulted as divine oracles. Sacred horses were deified because of their personal association with Divinities. Spiritual horses carried the human soul to Valhalla. Valuable horses were sacrificed to placate various gods. The story of Saint George *(left),* both as fact and legend, has come to symbolize the victory of good over evil. A religious equine taboo enacted in the 8th century AD still influences the dietary habits of modern Americans and Europeans today. *(cited from: http://www.lrgaf.org/articles/religion.htm)*

The White Horse Temple

White Horse Temple, boasting great antique architecture has remained intact for over 1,900 years.

In the year 64 of the Eastern Han Dynasty, Emperor Ming sent a delegation of his men to study Buddhism in the western world. After three years, two eminent Indian monks, She Moteng and Zhu Falan, came back with the delegation. They brought with them a white horse carrying Buddhist sutras and Buddhist figures on its back. This was the first time that Buddhism appeared in China.

To express his thanks to the two monks and their white horse, the emperor ordered the building of a monastery which he named the White Horse Temple. During this time, the two monks were busy translating sutras in the temple until they completed the Chinese sutra 'Forty-two Chapter Sutra,' which attracted many monks and meant that the temple became a center for Buddhist activity in China. It is for this reason that the temple is honored as the 'Founder's Home' and the 'Cradle of Buddhism in China.'

(cited from:

Four Horses of the Apocalypse

The Four Horses of the Apocalypse are symbols that are in the Bible. Just before the four horsemen appear in Revelation 6, John shows us, Jesus, holding the title deed to earth in Revelation chapter 5. Jesus said that Satan is now the god of our world. Revelation is the story of how Jesus gets the title deed to his world back. The title deed is a rolled-up scroll sealed by seven drops of wax. As Jesus begins to undo each of the wax seals, events on earth really heat up. The first seals are often referred to as the Four Horsemen of the Apocalypse. The term "Apocalypse," means "Revelation."

Revelation 6:1-2: *I watched as the Lamb opened the first of the seven seals... I looked, and there before me was a white horse! Its rider held a bow, and he was given a crown, and he rode out as a conqueror bent on conquest. The first seal opens at the beginning of the final 7-year "tribulation" leading up to the second coming.* The white horse and rider represent three and a half years of peace followed by three and a half years of war represented by the bow. The Anti-Christ is the first of God's judgments on a Christ-rejecting world. He who claims to be a savior is really a "Trojan Horse."

Revelation 6:3-4: *When the Lamb opened the second seal... Another horse came out, a fiery red one. Its rider was given the power to take peace from the earth and to make men slay each other. To him was given a large sword. This rider takes peace from the earth.* The red horse represents war and bloodshed. Nation will rise against nation during the Tribulation and individuals against each other. It is a time of murder, assassination, bloodshed, revolution, and war.

Revelation 6:5-6: *So I looked, and behold, a black horse, and he who sat on it had a pair of scales in his hand. And I heard a voice in the midst of the four living creatures saying, 'A quart of wheat for a denarius, and three quarts of barley for a denarius; and do not harm the oil and the wine.* The black horse represents famine. It takes an entire day's wages just to buy a quart of wheat. "Balances" reveal scarcity. In these future days, the price of food will skyrocket while millions have no access to food.

Revelation 6:7-8: *And I looked, and there before me was a pale horse! Its rider was named Death, and Hades was following close behind him. They were given power over a fourth of the earth to kill by sword, famine, and plague, and by the wild beasts of the earth.* Death is the pale rider with Hades (hell) following behind. They will kill with the sword, hunger, disease, and wild beasts—the four judgments the Lord said he would send.
(cited from: https://www.crosswalk.com/special-coverage/end-times/what-are-the-four-horsemen-of-the-apocalypse.html)

White Horse of Uffington

The prehistoric White Horse of Uffington is one of the oldest hill figures in Britain and is believed to have inspired the creation of all the other white horse hill figures in the region. Mystery abounds the creation of the White Horse – who made it, when and why? Some historians believe the figure represents a horse goddess connected with the local Belgae tribe, others believe it is Celtic goddess Epona, protector of horses.

There are or were at least twenty-four of these hill figures in Britain, with no less than thirteen being in Wiltshire. The White Horse of Uffington is the only one with known prehistoric origin. Initially believed to date back to the Iron Age due to similar images found depicted on coins from that period, more recent dating by the Oxford Archaeological Unit placed the hill figure in the Bronze Age, some 3,000 years ago.

The original purpose of the figure is unknown. The horse, which can only be viewed from above or from an adjacent plateau in the distance, is unique in its features and this leads some to believe it represents the mythical dragon that St. George slain on the adjacent Dragon hill or even his horse. However, others believe it represents a Celtic horse goddess Epona, known to represent fertility, healing, and death. Epona had a counterpart in Britain, Rhiannon so the Uffington white horse may have been cut by adherents of a cult of the horse-goddess to be worshipped in religious ceremonies. Others believe it may have been the emblem of a local tribe, and have been cut as a totem or badge marking their land. Some believe the horse could have been cut by worshippers of the sun god Belinos who was associated with horses. He was sometimes depicted on horseback, and Bronze and Iron Age sun chariots were shown as being drawn by horses.

During the Second World War the figure, easily recognizable from the air, was covered over with turf and hedge trimmings so that Luftwaffe pilots could not use it for navigation during bombing raids. *(cited from: https://www.ancient-origins.net/ancient-places-europe/mystery-white-horse-uffington-001445)*

Kanthaka

Siddhartha was born in Nepal during the 4th century BC. While scholars agree that he did in fact live, the events of his life are still debated. According to the most widely known story of his life, after experimenting with different teachings for years, and finding none of them acceptable, Siddhartha spent a fateful night in deep meditation. During his meditation, all of the answers he had been seeking became clear, and he achieved full awareness, thereby becoming Buddha.

According to legend, Siddhartha was a prince born into power and privilege. When the Prince came into manhood, he was given a pure white horse named Kanthaka who escorted him wherever he went. Even as Siddhartha rode Kanthaka while learning war game exercises, things were carried out most delicately; a white sunshade was held above the young Prince day and night to protect him from cold, heat, dust, dirt, and dew, even while riding his horse. *(left)*

Siddhartha, mounted on Kanthaka, proved his capabilities as a warrior and won the hand of Princess Yasodhara. At the age of 29, the prince journeyed through his father's kingdom and witnessed sickness and cruelty for the first time, so he decided to leave behind his life of luxury and to seek enlightenment. According to legend, he stared out on his journey with Kanthaka and "the horse's hooves were muffled by the gods" to prevent the palace guards from knowing of his departure. When Siddhartha dismounted for the last time, to continue his spiritual journey on foot, Kanthaka died of a broken heart caused by the separation from the one he loved. Yet in the act of divine grace, the faithful horse was reincarnated as an enlightened human being. *(cited from: https://bradkronen.com/2016/05/14/the-lotus-blossom-awaits-to-bloom-the-mortal-life-of-prince-siddhartha/ and http://www.lrgaf.org/articles/religion.htm)*

The Horse in the Zodiac

Astrology is an ancient type of divination. According to this belief, stars, planets and the moon influence the lives of humans on earth according to the position of these celestial bodies at the time of a person's birth.

The horse is the seventh of the twelve animal signs associated with the Chinese Zodiac. The Years of the Horse include 1918, 1930, 1942, 1954, 1966, 1978, 1990, 2002, 2014 and 2026. Belief in the divinity of the horse led to the reverence of the animal as a village deity in certain parts of China. The horse is believed to represent the element of Fire (Huo), which symbolizes energy and enthusiasm. Persons born in the year of the horse are believed to possess certain character traits, such as strength and outgoing nature. *(cited from: http://www.lrgaf.org/articles/religion.htm)*

Martin of Tours

Martin of Tours *(right)* is the patron saint of the U.S. Army Quartermaster Corps, which has a medal in his name. Saint Martin of Tours was born around 316 AD in Savaria, Pannonia in what is now Hungary. Just before Martin was born, Christianity was legalized in the Roman Empire, and the bloody persecution of Christians soon came to an end. Martin's parents were pagans, but at the age of ten, Martin chose to respond to the call of the Gospel and become a Christian.

His father was a tribune, which is a high-ranking officer in the Imperial Horse Guard. Martin and his family went with his father when he was assigned to a post at Ticinum, in Northern Italy. It is here that Martin would grow up. At the age of fifteen, Martin was required to follow his father into the cavalry corps of the Roman military. Martin is believed to have served in Gaul, and also eventually Milan and Treves. Scholars think he served as part of the emperor's guard.

As a young soldier, Martin encountered a beggar in Amiens. The beggar was unclothed, and it was very cold. Martin removed his cloak, and with his sword, he cut it in half. He gave this half to the beggar and dressed in the remnant. That night, Martin had a vision in which Christ appeared to him. The vision spoke to him, "Martin, a mere catechumen has clothed me." A catechumen is one who is being instructed in the Christian faith. *(cited from: https://www.catholic.org/saints/saint.php?saint_id=81)*

Machad Mamangam

Kerala, in southern India, is the site of an important equine religious ceremony known as Machad Mamangam. Believed to be one of the oldest festivals in Kerala, according to legend it began when the local king wished to honor the goddess Kavil Ammaby by bringing valuable horses to the Thiruvanikkavu temple as an offering. There were no horses in his kingdom at that time, so the monarch and his subjects created enormous, highly decorated artificial horses instead. These large horse figurines are made from bamboo, filled with straw, and covered in colorful silk cloth. This unique five-day festival is held every three years. The culmination of the celebration occurs when men from nearby villages carry the five giant horses through the countryside to the temple. They are accompanied by musicians and thousands of joyful devotees who believe that the delivery of the horses to the goddess will ensure prosperity and harmony. *(cited from: http://www.lrgaf.org/articles/religion.htm)*

The Horse in Islam

Horses are mentioned in the Qu'ran six times. The Muslim holy book explains that Allah created horses, known as "El-Kheir," the supreme blessing, for humanity's benefit and pleasure. "Allah created the horse from the wind as he created Adam from clay. He said to the south wind, 'I want to make a creature out of you. Condense,' and the wind condensed. Allah said to the horse, 'I will make you peerless and preferred above all the other animals and tenderness will always be in your master's heart. You alone shall fly without wings. All the blessings of the world shall be placed between your eyes and happiness shall hang from your forelock.'"

An Ayat *(above)* is a portion of the Qu'ran. Islamic calligraphers were renowned for their ability to transmit an ayat in various artistic forms. Ayat al-Kursi, (The Throne Verse), Surah 2:255, was transformed into an equine form by a Mughal calligrapher in the 16th century. (*cited from: http://www.lrgaf.org/articles/religion.htm*)

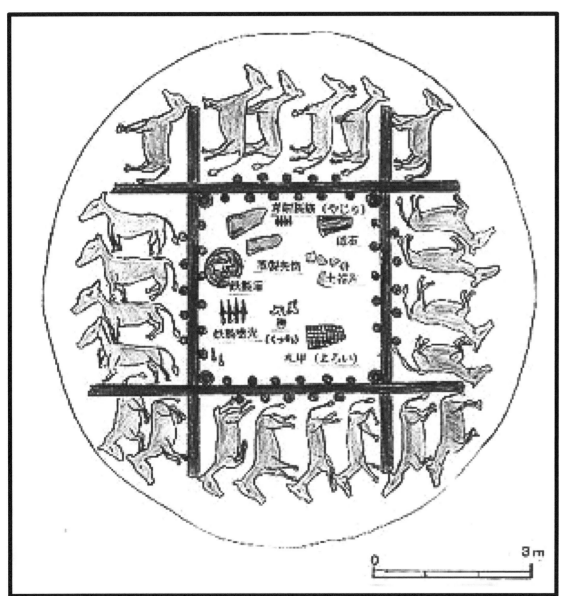

0   3 m

Scythian Horses

The Scythians were a nomadic equestrian tribe that inhabited the Eurasian steppes beginning in the 9th century BC. These Bronze Age people were among the earliest people to become accomplished mounted warriors. They also believed in gods and goddesses, including Gaia, the female personification of the Earth, who would meet them in the afterlife. One important religious practice was horse burial. When a rich tribal chief died, he would be placed inside a wooden log building. Alongside his body would be placed opulent treasures. Prized horses would be killed and laid along the outside of the building. The entire affair was then covered with earth and a large mound, known as a kurgan, would mark the spot of the chief's departure to Otherworld. In 1897 a Russian archaeologist excavated the kurgan of a Scythian chief who had died in the 7th century BC. The sketch *(left)* drawn by N.I. Veselovski depicts how twenty-two horses had been carefully placed around the departed chief's body. (*cited from: http://www.lrgaf.org/articles/religion.htm*)

The Horses of Shinto

Shinto, (the way of the gods) is the traditional religion of Japan. It involves the worship of numerous spirits known as kami. These spirits manifest themselves in various forms including rocks, trees, places, and animals. The white stallion is a sacred creature in Shinto. According to the Nihongi Chronicles (720 BC), when a member of the Imperial Family died, his holdings, retainers, and horses were interred alive with him. Emperor Suinin ended this practice, reasoning that it was more humane to use clay figurines representing the assets of the deceased than to bury the real ones. People began to offer live horses to the shrines. This created two conflicts. What could the priests do with so many live horses? And spiritual anguish was experienced by those devotees who were too poor to offer an expensive animal. Around the 8th century, instead of living animals, the faithful began using small tablets with a picture of a horse as a votive gift.

By the Heian period (794-1185 AD) the horse was viewed by the nobility as more of an elegant accessory than a weapon of war. Commoners relied on the horse as an agricultural partner and a traveling companion. Hatsuuma, the First Horse-Day-Festival, is one of the best examples of an association of the Divine Horse with the agricultural base of the nation. A 711 AD legend says that, on the Day of the Horse, in Fushimi, Kyoto, the God of Agriculture, business and prosperity, Inari, descended from the mountain. Currently, all throughout Japan, the god's devotees visit his shrines, to pay their respects. They come accompanied by horses elaborately decorated; *(above),* or they offer prayers on top of straw horses. *(right)* (*cited from: http://www.lrgaf.org/articles/religion.htm*)

Al Borak

Mohammed's personal horse was named Al Borak, which means "lightning" in Arabic. This mythical white-winged mare was said to have a human head, thus proving the ancient metaphysical belief that horses and men were once joined. *(left)* After Muhammad's death in 632 AD, his followers said that he was borne to the Seventh Heaven on the back of Al Borak. *(cited from: http://www.alborak-arabians.com/alborak_legend_story.htm)*

Mohammed and the Five Mares

When the prophet Mohammed was traveling across the desert with the Bedouin, hundreds of camels and horses traveled with them. One day Mohammed announced that for three days and nights, he would forbid the horses to drink even a drop of water. "How can you do such a thing?" the people cried. "Wasn't it you who told us every man shall love his horse?" "Yes," said Mohammed, "but it is the will of Allah." It was the height of summer, and the heat wafted up from the sands and poured down from the sun. The horses were faint and dizzy with thirst, and the people begged Mohammed. "Please, let the horses drink." The prophet refused. "Allah commands me to make this test," he explained.

At long last, the end of the third day came, and just as the moon began to rise, Mohammed lifted the horn that hung at the entrance to his tent and walked to the place where he had ordered the horses be kept enclosed. As he approached, the horses looked longingly toward the nearby watering hole, then their eyes traveled to Mohammed's face. Their bodies shivered in anticipation. Would he set them free at last? Their nostrils quivered. They watched intently as he walked to the gate. And then he unlatched that gate. Hundreds of parched horses, desperate to drink, raced as one out of that enclosure, and for a moment they looked to be only a swirl of howling dust. As they galloped toward the watering hole, their tails whirling, they seemed almost to fly. But just before the first horse reached the water, Mohammed raised the horn to his lips and blew into it. This was the call to war. The horses had been trained to stop at that sound, to come at once to their master. This, they knew, was their sacred duty. But the horses ignored the call. Some say they could not hear it over the thundering hooves and pounding hearts. They nearly crushed each other in that mad stampede to the cool oasis. They carried on, and the first to reach it dipped their heads and drank as if they would never stop, edging away only when another desperate creature pushed its way in.

But five horses did hear that trumpeting sound. Five mares stopped, turned around and faced their master. Five mares gave up the dream of that fresh, cool water. Five mares walked toward their master and stood before him, ready to obey his will, no matter what it was. Mohammed knew that these were the five mares that were most worthy of Allah. These, then, were the five mares who would carry Allah's name to every corner of the Earth, the five who would foal the finest horses in the entire world. He patted their silky manes, and he studied them. Their foreheads were large, he saw. Surely this was because those foreheads held the blessings of Allah. Their high-tailed carriages symbolized the pride of greatness, and their arched necks and high crests showed their remarkable spirit. "You are creatures of the great Allah," he said, "and you will forever be special." Then he led them to the watering hole to quench their thirst, and as he watched them, he had tears of joy in his eyes.

People say it is from these five horses that the five breeds of Arabian horses, Al Khamsa, descend. The five families -- Kehilan, Seglawi, Abeyan, Hamdani, and Hadban -- each possess the loyalty and courage of those five mares who passed the test of Mohammed.

Horses in Folk Tales, Fables and Legends

Storytelling is common to every culture. Most people enjoy listening to stories. Legends, Folk Tales and Fables are all popular methods of storytelling.

A Legend is a semi-true story, which has been passed on from person-to-person and has significant meaning or symbolism for the culture in which it originates

A Folktale is a popular story that was passed on in spoken form, from one generation to the next. Usually, the author is unknown, and there are often many versions of the tale

Fables usually have talking animals and teach a lesson. Fables are short and often have only 2 or 3 characters

(Cited from: http://myths.e2bn.org/teachers/info311-what-are-myths-legends-and-folktales.html)

Bayard

Bayard is the name of a horse found in the legends of Charlemagne. Although looking like an average horse, Bayard could stretch its back to accommodate all four of the sons of Aymon. Bayard was also known for possessing great speed. To win the horse, it was necessary to conquer him by force or skill, this rendering him tame and docile. In the legend, Renaud, one of the four sons of Aymon, is forced to cede Bayard to Charlemagne who, as punishment for the horse's exploits, has a large stone tied to Bayard's neck and has the horse pushed into the river; Bayard, however, smashes the stone with his hooves and escapes to live forever more in the woods.

Bayard often appears in literature including Chaucer's Canterbury Tales. Statues of Bayard are often found in towns in Belgium. Outside the town of Dinant stands "Bayard rock," a large cleft rock formation that was said to have been split by Bayard's mighty hooves. In the next town down the river, Namur, there is a statue of Bayard and the four Aymon Brothers along the River Meuse. There are many places in Wallonia region of Belgium linked to the legend of the 4fourAymon Brothers and Bayard. *(cited from: https://www.revolvy.com/page/Bayard-%28legend%29)*

36

King Soloman, Ishmael and the Arabian Horse

Another tale of the origin of the Arabian horse tells that King Solomon gave his famous stallion, Zad el-Raheb or Zad-el-Rakib ("Gift to the Rider") to the Banu Azd people when they came to pay tribute to the king. This legendary stallion was said to be faster than the zebra and the gazelle, and every hunt with him was successful. Thus the Arabs put him to stud, and he became a founding sire of legend.

Yet another creation story puts the origin of the Arabian in the time of Ishmael, the son of Abraham. In this story, the Angel Jibril (also known as Gabriel) descended from Heaven and awakened Ishmael with a "wind-spout" that whirled toward him. The Angel then commanded the thundercloud to stop scattering dust and rain, and so it gathered itself into a prancing, handsome creature - a horse - that seemed to swallow up the ground. Hence, the Bedouins bestowed the title "Drinker of the Wind" to the first Arabian horse. *(cited from The Al Thumama Stud Facebook page)*

The Bedouin and the Arabian Horse

Bedouins are a group of nomadic Arabian people. Bedouins have been referred to by various names throughout history, including Qedarites in the Old Testament. Qedarites are named for Qedar, the second son of Ishmael, mentioned in the Bible's books of Genesis and Chronicles. Bedouins have often been associated with the origins of the Arabian horse. They believed that the Arabian horse was a gift to them from their Creator, to be cherished and protected as a member of the household. *(left)* Therefore, for more than a thousand years, it was a matter of honor for the Bedouin, as well as a safeguard for their continued existence, to breed their horses pure as defined by their own strict standards. The harsh environment of the Bedouins perfected the characteristics of the Arabian horse. The Arabian horse became the ideal instrument of war: swift, responsive, agile and enduring, with courage, loyalty and the ability to withstand privation. The need to maintain the breed in this form was confirmed by the Bedouin's constant struggle for survival in the desert and by inter-tribal warfare.

(cited from: https://arabianhorse.savvity.net/articles/59248f9e1d41c867c303b663-horse-of-the-bedouin)

Cheval Mallet

It is said that in ancient times, a fabulously beautiful but evil horse sometimes appeared in the evening or in the middle of the night, white as fog, well saddled and bridled, to tempt the traveler exhausted by a long journey. This happened most often on a moonless night. Then the weary traveler was tempted and rode on this mount. Immediately, the horse began to gallop without anyone being able to stop it, like a raging hurricane, smoking nostrils and sparkling eyes illuminating the horizon. His fantastic ride always ended in the morning with the death of the horseman, who, thrown to the ground, died instantly or was trampled to death by the horse, then thrown into a precipice or a fountain. Close to the body, strangely shaped hoof prints were often found.

Front   **Back**

The only truly effective protection was a medal of Saint Benedict (called "cross of sorcerers"). *(left)* The letters (VRSNSMVSVQLIVB) that appear around this medal protect from perils. These letters are meant to mean "Vade retro, Satana; No suadeas mihi vana; suntvana quae libas; ipse venena bibas '" (Get away Satan! Do not suggest me your vanities; bad things are what you offer, Drink your poison yourself!) These letters correspond to an exorcism prayer based on an incident in the life of St. Benedict. The incident happened like this: After St. Benedict had been a hermit for three years, and his reputation for holiness had spread everywhere, a group of monks came to ask them to be his abbot. San Benedict agreed, but some rebellious monks of that community really did not like this idea and decided to kill Saint Benedict by poisoning his bread and wine. As Saint Benedict made the sign of the cross over his food, as was his custom, the cup was immediately broken, and he knew then that his food had been poisoned. He threw the wine on the ground, saying: Vade retro, Satana; No suadeas mihi vana; suntvana quae libas; ipse venena bibas *(cited from: https://www.accueil-vendee.com/decouvertes/legende-du-cheval-mallet and http://www.padrerafa.com/la-medalla-de-san-benito-asombrosa-arma-para-el-combate-espiritual)*

Gringolet

In the medieval tales of King Arthur and his knights of the Round Table, "Gringolet" was the loyal steed of Sir Gawain, who was either Arthur's greatest knight (if you believe the English), or second-greatest knight after Sir Lancelot (if you believe the French).

Gringolet is a male horse and is almost always described as a charger, in other words, the generic term for a horse specifically bred and trained for use in mounted combat. When a color is given for Gringolet, he is usually described as pure white in color, which is an obvious symbol of Sir Gawain's purity as a knight.

Gringolet's earliest known appearance as the name of Gawain's horse is in Chrétien de Troyes' late-12th century French romance Erec and Enide. In Erec and Enide Gawain loans Gringolet to Sir Kay to joust against Erec. However even Gringolet's might cannot save the incompetent Sir Kay from defeat at the hands of Erec, who after all is the hero of that tale. Chrétien's romances were incredibly influential, and "Gringolet" became the canonical name for Sir Gawain's horse in all later Arthurian romances.

In the romances, there was no consensus on Gringolet's origin story. In the Vulgate Cycle, Sir Gawain wins him in a contest with a Saxon warrior, but in Wolfram von Eschenbach's German romance Parzival, Sir Gawain discovers him in the sacred stables of the Grail Castle.

The name "Gringolet" is of unknown origin as well. Many of the French names for Arthurian characters were derived from earlier Celtic forms, so it may have been that the name "Gringolet" derived from some sort of pre-Chrétien Brythonic tradition now lost, and in light of this possibility scholars have suggested two possible derivations from Welsh – "Gwyn Caled" meaning "white hardy" or "Cein Caled" meaning "handsome hardy." *(cited from: https://everything2.com/title/Gringolet)*

(cited from: https://clasmerdin.blogspot.com/2014/01/afanc-water-demon.html)

Llamrei

Llamrei *(left)* was a mare owned by King Arthur, according to the Welsh tale "Culhwch and Olwen."

Situated high above the northern banks of the River Dyfi is Llyn Barfog, the Bearded Lake. It is said that a terrible water demon, the Afanc, lived in the lake, from where it would raid the surrounding countryside. The Afanc would kill anybody who went close to Llyn Barfog where it had made its home. Sometimes it went on the rampage, killing people in the town and causing flood damage as it thrashed around in the lake. When Arthur came to hear of the strife caused by the water demon at Llyn Barfog he went to the lake and threw a great chain around the Afanc. Using his horse Llamrei to pull the Afanc from the lake, the struggle was so arduous that his steed left a hoof print in a nearby rock overlooking the Dovey Estuary.

Today a stone on a hill above Aber-tafol, Merioneth, on the A493, bears a depression that is said to be the hoofprint of Arthur's horse, known locally as Carreg Carn March Arthur (Stone of Arthur's Steed's Hoof). *(right)*

40

Pecos Bill is a cowboy of American folk tales. Dynamite was said to be his favorite food. Pecos used a rattlesnake named Shake as a lasso. His horse, Widow-Maker (also called Lightning), was so named because no other man could ride him and live. Widowmaker is first introduced in the tales crossing a desert with vultures circling above him. The young horse tries to defend himself but is quickly overwhelmed due to his thirst. However, Bill arrives in time and saves Widowmaker from the vultures. Since then, the pair became inseparable.

In the years that followed, Widowmaker and Bill accomplished many achievements, from lassoing evil rustlers, to digging up the Rio Grande and creating the Painted Desert. One day, as they were butting heads with buffalo, they meet the beautiful redheaded cowgirl Slue-Foot Sue, who immediately captures the attention of Pecos Bill while riding on her giant catfish down a river. Bill's eccentric behavior confuses Widowmaker at first until he realizes that the cowboy has fallen in love with the young girl and he starts to cry. During that evening, as Bill successfully woos Sue, Widowmaker weeps over the thought of losing his closest friend.

On Bill and Sue's wedding day, as Bill excitedly waits for Sue, several other cowboys with ropes are holding down Widowmaker, who is now in a fit of jealousy over Sue taking Bill away from him. Sue begs Pecos to let her ride him. When Sue sits on his back wearing her yellow gown and bustle, he attempts to throw Sue off. Surprisingly, Sue is able to stay on Widowmaker for a while, despite him bucking so much that his horseshoes come off. But while Sue calmly powders her face during her rough ride, her bustle suddenly begins to bounce repeatedly. Widowmaker continues to buck Sue's bustle, sending her higher and higher until the leather reins tear in half. As Sue bounces up into the sky over and over again, Bill attempts to lasso her down. Unknown to Bill and the others, Widowmaker stands on the rope whistling innocently, causing Bill to miss and Sue to land on the moon. After that, a distraught Bill and Widowmaker return to live with the coyote pack. *(cited from: http://disney.wikia.com/wiki/Widowmaker)*

The Charger and the Ass

A charger adorned with fine trappings came thundering along the road, exciting the envy of a poor ass who was trudging along the same way with a heavy load on his back. "Get out of my road!" said the proud horse, "or I shall trample you under my feet." The ass said nothing but quietly moved on one side to let the horse pass.

Not long afterward the charger was engaged in the wars and, being badly wounded in battle, was rendered unfit for military service and sent to work upon a farm. When the ass saw him dragging with great labor a heavy wagon, he understood how little reason he had had to envy one who, by his overbearing spirit in the time of his prosperity, had lost those friends who might have succored him in time of need.

Moral: Be not hasty to envy the condition of others.

The Horse and His Rider

A soldier took the utmost pains with his charger. As long as the war lasted, he looked upon him as his fellow-helper in all emergencies and fed him carefully with hay and corn. When the war was over, he only allowed him chaff to eat, made him carry heavy loads of wood, and subjected him to much slavish drudgery and ill-treatment.

War, however, once again proclaimed, and the trumpet summoning him to his standard, the soldier put on his charger the military trappings and mounted in his heavy coat of mail. The horse fell down straightway under the weight, no longer equal to the burden, and said to his master, "You must now go to the war on foot, for you have transformed me from a horse into an ass and how can you expect that I can again turn in a moment from an ass to a horse?"

Moral: He who slights his friends when they are not needed must not expect them to serve him when he needs them

42

The Horse and the Groom

A groom who used to steal and sell a horse's corn was yet very busy in grooming and wisping him all day long. "If you really wish me," said the horse, "to look well, give me less of your currying and more of your corn."

Moral: If you wish to do a service, do it right.

The Horse and the Loaded Ass

A man who kept a horse and an ass was wont in his journeys to spare the horse and put the entire burden upon the ass' back. The ass, who had been ailing for some time, besought the horse one day to relieve him of part of his load. "For if," said he, "you would take a fair portion, I shall soon get well again; but if you refuse to help me, this weight will kill me." The horse, however, bade the ass get on and not trouble him with his complaints. The ass jogged on in silence, but presently, overcome with the weight of his burden, dropped down dead, as he had foretold. Upon this, the master unloosed the load from the dead ass and, putting it upon the horse's back, made him carry the ass' carcass in addition.
"Alas, for my ill nature!" said the horse. "By refusing to bear my just portion of the load, I have now to carry the whole of it, with a dead weight in the bargain."

Moral: A disobliging temper carries its own punishment.

The Horse and the Stag

A horse had the whole range of a meadow to himself, but a stag came and damaged the pasture. The horse, anxious to have his revenge, asked a man if he could not assist him in punishing the stag. "Yes," said the man, "only let me put a bit in your mouth and get up on your back, and I will find the weapons." The horse agreed, and the man mounted accordingly. But instead of getting his revenge, the horse has been from that time forward the slave of man.

Moral: Revenge is too dearly purchased at the price of liberty.

The Man, the Horse, the Ox, and the Dog

A horse, ox, and dog, driven to great straits by the cold, sought shelter and protection from a man. He received them kindly, lighted a fire, and warmed them. He allowed the horse to eat of his oats, gave the ox an abundance of hay and fed the dog with meat from his own table.

Grateful for these favors, they determined to repay him to the best of their ability. They divided for this purpose the term of his life between them, and each endowed one portion of it with the qualities that chiefly characterized himself.

The horse chose the man's earliest years and endowed them with his own attributes. Hence every man is in youth impetuous, headstrong, and obstinate in maintaining his own opinion.

The ox took under his patronage the next term of life, and therefore man in his middle age is fond of work, devoted to labor and resolute to amass wealth and to husband his resources.

The end of life was reserved to the dog, wherefore the old man is often snappish, irritable, hard to please and selfish, tolerant only of his own household, but averse to strangers and to all who do not administer to his comfort or to his necessities.

Moral: No act of kindness, no matter how small, is ever wasted.

The Wolf and the Horse

As a wolf was roaming over a farm, he came to a field of oats. Not being able to eat them, he left them and went his way. Presently meeting with a horse, he bade him come with him into the field; "For," says he, "I have found some capital oats, and I have not tasted one, but have kept them all for you, for the very sound of your teeth is music to my ear." But the horse replied, "A pretty fellow! If wolves were able to eat oats, I suspect you would not have preferred your ears to your appetite."

Moral: Little thanks are due to him who only gives away what is of no use to himself.

The Charger and the Miller

A Horse, who had been used to carry his rider into battle, felt himself growing old and chose to work in a mill instead. He now no longer found himself stepping out proudly to the beating of the drums, but was compelled to slave away all day grinding the corn. Bewailing his hard lot, he said one day to the Miller, "Ah me! I was once a splendid war-horse, gaily caparisoned, and attended by a groom whose sole duty was to see to my wants. How different is my present condition! I wish I had never given up the battlefield for the mill." The Miller replied with asperity, "It's no use your regretting the past. Fortune has many ups and downs: you must just take them as they come."

Moral: Fortune has its ups and downs.

The Fox, the Wolf, and the Horse

A Fox seeing a Horse for the first time grazing in a field, at once ran to a Wolf of his acquaintance and described the animal that he had found. "It is, perhaps," said the Fox, "some delicious prey that fortune has put in our path. Come with me, and judge for yourself." Off they ran and soon came to the Horse, who, scarcely lifting his head, seemed little anxious to be on speaking terms with such suspicious-looking characters. "Sir," said the Fox, "your humble servants here would with pleasure learn the name by which you are known to your illustrious friends." The Horse, who was not without a ready wit, said his name was there curiously written upon his hoofs for the information of those who cared to read it. "Gladly would I," replied the sly fox, suspecting in an instant something wrong, "but my parents were poor, and could not pay for my education; hence, I never learned to read. The friends of my companion here, on the contrary, are great folk, and he can both read and write, and has a thousand other accomplishments." The Wolf, pleased with the flattery, at once went up, with a knowing air, to examine one of the hoofs which the Horse raised for his convenience; and when he had come near enough, the Horse gave a sudden and vigorous kick, and back to earth fell the Wolf, his jaw broken and bleeding. "Well, cousin," cried the Fox, with a grin, "you need never ask for the name a second time, now that you have it written so plainly just below your eyes."

Moral: Friends may turn on you.

The Honest Horse

A story goes that Caligula, Emperor of Rome, was one day on the back of a favorite horse, with his whole court mulling about him. These obsequious gentlemen, perceiving how awkwardly he managed the reins, took occasion from thence to flatter him. Saying he was a most excellent horseman. Whereupon the horse immediately threw him off. The Emperor, perceiving that the horse was the only one of his court that had any truth in him, took a resolution to raise him to those high honors to which he afterward arrived.

Moral: The honest man carries preference in esteem.

The Horse and the Lion

A Lion, who had got old and infirm, saw a fine plump nag and longed for a bit of him. Knowing that the animal would prove too fleet for him in the chase, he had recourse to artifice. He gave out to all the beasts that, having spent many years in studying physic, he was now prepared to heal any malady or distemper with which they might be afflicted. He hoped by that means to get admittance among them, and so find a chance of gratifying his appetite. The horse, who had doubts of the Lion's honesty, came up limping, pretending that he had run a thorn into one of his hind feet, which gave him great pain. The lion asked that the foot might be shown to him, and pored over it with a mock earnest air. The horse, slyly looking around, saw that he was preparing to spring, and vigorously sending out both his heels at once, gave the Lion such a kick in the face, that it laid him stunned and sprawling upon the ground. Then laughing at the success of his trick, he trotted merrily away.

Moral: Fooling those trying to fool you is beneficial.

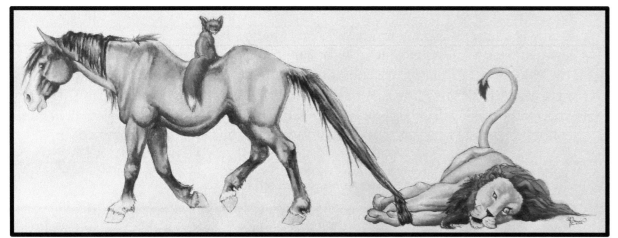

A peasant had a faithful horse which had grown old and could do no more work. So his master no longer wanted to give him anything to eat. He said, "I can certainly make no more use of you, but still I mean well by you, and if you prove yourself still strong enough to bring me a lion here, I will maintain you. But for now, get out of my stable." With that, he chased him into the open field.

The horse was sad and went to the forest to seek a little protection there from the weather. There the fox met him and said, "Why do you hang your head so, and go about all alone?" "Alas," replied the horse, "greed and loyalty do not dwell together in one house. My master has forgotten what services I have performed for him for so many years, and because I can no longer plow well, he will give me no more food, and has driven me out." "Without giving you a chance?" asked the fox. "The chance was a bad one. He said, if I were still strong enough to bring him a lion, he would keep me, but he well knows that I cannot do that." The fox said, "I will help you. Just lie down, stretch out as if you were dead, and do not stir."

The horse did what the fox asked, and then the fox went to the lion, who had his den not far off, and said, "A dead horse is lying out there. Just come with me, and you can have a rich meal." The lion went with him, and when they were both standing by the horse the fox said, "After all, it is not very comfortable for you here -- I tell you what -- I will fasten it to you by the tail, and then you can drag it into your cave and eat it in peace." This advice pleased the lion. He positioned himself, and so that the fox might tie the horse fast to him, he kept completely quiet. But the fox tied the lion's legs together with the horse's tail and twisted and fastened everything so well and so strongly that no amount of strength could pull it loose. When he had finished his work, he tapped the horse on the shoulder and said, "Pull, white horse, pull!"

Then up sprang the horse at once, and pulled the lion away with him. The lion began to roar so that all the birds in the forest flew up in terror, but the horse let him roar, and drew him and dragged him across the field to his master's door. When the master saw the lion, he was of a better mind, and said to the horse, "You shall stay with me and farewell." And he gave him plenty to eat until he died.

The White Horse

A Cree chief had a lovely daughter who was sought after by many brave warriors. Two suitors led the rivalry for her hand, a Cree chief from Lake Winnipegosis and a Sioux chief from Devil's Lake. The girl herself favored the Cree warrior, and when he brought a beautiful white horse from Mexico as a gift for her father, the man agreed to the marriage.

The Sioux chief was enraged by the rejection of his suit. On the day of the wedding, he gathered a war-party and came thundering across the plains toward the home of the beautiful maiden. The Cree chief tossed his lovely bride on top of the white horse and leaped upon his own gray steed. The couple fled to the west with the rejected Sioux and his war-party on their heels.

The canny Cree chief doubled back several times, and the couple hid among the prairie bluffs. For a time, it seemed as if they had lost the Sioux. But once they were on the plains again, the beautiful white horse was visible for miles, and the war party soon found them. A rain of arrows fell upon the fleeing lovers, and the warrior and his bride fell dead from their mounts. At once, the Sioux captured the gray steed, but the white horse evaded them. One man claimed he saw the spirit of the young bride enter into the horse just before it fled from their clutches.

The white horse roamed the prairies for many years following the death of the Cree warrior and his lovely bride. The inhabitants feared to approach the horse since the spirit of the maiden dwelled within it. Long after its physical body passed away, the soul of the white horse continued to gallop across the plains, and the land where it roamed became known as the White Horse Plain. They say that the soul of the white horse continues to haunt the prairie to this very day.

A statue of the white horse was erected at St. Francois Xavier on the Trans-Canada Highway west of Winnipeg, to remind all who see it of the phantom white horse and the beautiful maiden who once rode it. *(cited from: http://americanfolklore.net/folklore/2010/07/post_1.html)*

49

The Ghost Stallion – A Yinnuwok Legend

Long ago, The Traveler was a wealthy chief. A warrior in his young days, he had taken many scalps, many horses and many trophies of value. He had increased his possessions by hard dealings with those less fortunate and by gambling with younger men who were no match for his cunning. He was not loved by his fellow tribesmen -- though they admired his bravery -- for in times of hardship when other chiefs shared freely whatever they had, he drove hard bargains and generally prospered from the ills of others. His wives he had abused till their parents took them away, his children hated him, and he had no love for them.

One morning, when he went to the little valley in which his horses were kept, he found in the herd an ugly white stallion. He was old, with crooked legs, and a matted coat, thin, and tired looking. The Traveler flew into a rage. He took his rawhide rope and caught the poor old horse. Then, with a club, he beat him unmercifully. When the animal fell to the ground, stunned, The Traveler broke his legs with the club and left him to die. He returned to his lodge, feeling not the slightest remorse for his cruelty. Later, deciding he might as well have the hide of the old horse, he returned to the place where he had left him. But, to his surprise, the white stallion was gone.

That night, as The Traveler slept, he had a dream. The white stallion appeared to him and slowly turned into a beautiful horse, shining white, with long mane and tail - a horse lovelier than any The Traveler had ever seen. Then the Stallion spoke: "If you had treated me kindly," the stallion said, "I would have brought you more horses. You were cruel to me, so I shall take away the horses you have!"

When The Traveler awoke, he found his horses were gone. All that day, he walked and searched, but when at nightfall he fell asleep exhausted, he had found no trace of them. In his dreams, the White Stallion came again, and said, "Do you wish to find your horses? They are north, by a lake. You will sleep twice before you come to it." As soon as he awakened in the morning, The Traveler hastened northward. Two days' journey, and when he came to the lake there were no horses. That night, the Ghost Stallion came again. "Do you wish to find your horses?" he said. "They are east, in some hills. There will be two sleeps before you came to the place." When the sun had gone down on the third day, The Traveler had searched the hills but had found no horses. So it went night after night the Stallion came to The Traveler, directing him to some distant spot, but he never found his horses. He grew thin, and footsore. Sometimes he got a horse from some friendly camp, sometimes he stole one, in the night. But always, before morning, would come loud drumming of hoofs, the Ghost Stallion and his band would gallop by, and the horse of The Traveler would break its picket, and go with them. Never again did he have a horse. Never again did he see his own lodge. He wanders, even to this day, the old men say, still searching for his lost horses. Sometimes, they say, on a windy autumn night when the stars shine very clearly, and over on the Cree Jump the coyotes howl, above the wind you may hear a rush of running horses, and the stumbling footsteps of an old man and you may see the Stallion and his band--and The Traveler, still pursuing them, still trying to get back his beautiful horses. *(cited from: https://www.manataka.org/page2275.html)*

In the beginning, there was only the Sun and Earth. There was a woman who lived on the Earth, who rode a white horse named N'Tuki, meaning 'spirited one'; and her rider was named Fa'Rashi, meaning 'spirited rider.'

This particular horse was special; for when it was to die, it would be cast into the heavens for all humans to see. Fa'Rashi's job was to keep this horse clean; to preserve its white coat until it died. So, every time she took N'Tuki out riding, she would return and immediately wash her so that no mud-stains defiled her white coat.

N'Tuki got pregnant, and five months later she bore a filly, just as white as her mother. But tragedy befell N'Tuki that day; she died during childbirth, and Fa'Rashi saw N'Tuki's spirit rise into the night-air and sprinkle among the heavens; she became the stars. Then Fa'Rashi heard the voice of a God, it said: "Your task now is to keep N'Tuki's child free from any blemishes that might stain her white coat; for when she dies, she shall be cast into the heavens for all humans to see. If you do this, you shall await a similar fate."

So every time she took N'Tuki's daughter, N'Kuki, meaning 'young spirited one,' out riding, she would return and wash her immediately so that no mud-stains defiled her white coat.

But one day, Fa'Rashi took N'Kuki out riding in the night to look at the stars; this proved not to be a smart idea. Fa'Rashi wanted to feel the summer-air rush past her; through her hair and behind her ears, so she urged her horse to ride faster and faster. But Fa'Rashi could not see where she was going, and they plummeted into a ditch, covering N'Kuki's left side with mud. Three of her legs were injured, and Fa'Rashi was unconscious.

N'Kuki knew what to do. She climbed out of the ditch and galloped to their home, each stride weakening her legs and deepening her pain. N'Kuki quickly picked up a sack of healing herbs from the teepee with her teeth and started for Fa'Rashi; her legs killing her but she rode on. Presently, she was limping along when she stumbled over the depression at the edge of the ditch; her legs crumbling beneath her. N'Kuki slid next to Fa'Rashi and chewed the herbs into a paste, then administered it with her lips onto Fa'Rashi's wounds; she fainted just after.

In the morning, Fa'Rashi awoke in good health but only to find N'Kuki had died saving her life. She spent the day in mourning and awaited the night. When night came, she gazed upon the stars and found a brighter, larger one among them. N'Kuki had become the moon, but she was not pure; for it is easily seen that on one side, she is wrought with spots and stains and because Fa'Rashi faulted in her duty, she will not join the moon and the stars. *(cited from: https://urbanlegendsonline.com/legend-of-the-spirited-horse/)*

Horses that Became Legendary

A legendary horse is worth remembering throughout years to come even after the horse has died. A legendary horse has attained this status because it leaves an unforgettable mark in some way. Their story is told over and over again and is remembered throughout history leaving a legacy for others to remember. *(left – Winchester aka Rienzi with General Phillip Sheridan The equestrian statue is located in the center of Sheridan Circle in the Sheridan-Kalorama neighborhood of Washington, D.C.)*

Rienzi – Winchester

WINCHESTER (aka Rienzi) (ca. 1858-1878) *(left)* was General Philip Sheridan's horse. He was a jet-black stallion with three white socks. Winchester / Rienzi was foaled in Grand Rapids, Michigan. His bloodline included Morgan horses of the prestigious Black Hawk line. He had a long stride and walked at roughly five mph. At more than 16 hands high, he was big for the slightly built General Sheridan. Sheridan rode Winchester/Rienzi almost continuously for the next three years -- through fort five engagements and nineteen fierce battles and cavalry raids. Winchester/Rienzi became a national celebrity in October 1864 when he played a role in saving the Union Army from defeat at Cedar Creek. Sheridan was in Washington DC for a staff meeting, when Confederates launched a surprise attack on his troops in Cedar Creek Virginia.

Sheridan was still twenty miles away in Winchester when he awoke to the sound of cannons. Sheridan rode Rienzi at full gallop towards his troops arriving in time to rally his soldiers: "Men, by God, we'll whip them yet!" he shouted. Sheridan's troops rallied and prevailed. In the poem, "Sheridan's Ride," Thomas Buchanan Read tells the story of the most dramatic ride in military history. The historic ride created a media frenzy and inspired paintings, prints, songs, and monuments. Henceforth, Rienzi became nationally known as Winchester. After his death in October 1878, Winchester was preserved and mounted and is on display at the National Museum of American History. *(right)*

Babieca

El Cid, born Rodrigo Díaz de Vivar (1043–1099) was a Castilian nobleman during the reign of Emperor Ferdinand the Great. He is considered to be the National Hero of Spain for his bravery and military genius on the battlefield. His equally famous horse was Babieca. Exactly how much of the tale of the two warriors is myth or historical fact is unknown, but we do know that El Cid and Babieca were indeed war heroes, and their tombs remain intact to this day. A true man of Spain, during his lifetime he fought against both the Christian kings and the Muslim invaders, most notably, retaking Valencia, and many years later, saving it from a siege in his most famous battle.

The legend begins with young Rodrigo coming of age. As a gift, his uncle, a Carthusian monk by the name of Pedro El Grande, bade him select a young colt from his stables. Of all the fine Carthusian colts, Rodrigo selected what his uncle considered to be a weak and inferior animal, and exclaimed "Babieca!", or "Stupid!". The name stuck, but the gray colt grew into a fine white war horse, a typical Carthusian horse noted for his docility, loyalty, striking appearance, and nimble feet.

El Cid was noted for his unusual tactical brilliance. His plans were immaculate, and his ability to inspire courage in his troops and terror in his enemies became famous far and wide. Modern generals describe some of his tactics as psychological warfare which El Cid used to great advantage. He insisted upon having Roman books on military tactics read aloud to his unlettered troops both to boost their morale as well as to educate them. He accepted suggestions and ideas from his troops as well, another unusual strategy.

However, the story that truly elevated El Cid and fearless Babieca into legends was said to have happened after the El Cid's death during the siege of Valencia. El Cid was killed; today it is not known exactly what killed him. Regardless, his men were in dire straits without their leader to inspire fear in the hearts of their enemies and courage in their troops. Drawing from his almost otherworldly reputation, legend has it that they strapped his fully armored body to Babieca's saddle and fixed his right arm pointing into the air, grasping his sword. The invaders, hearing of his death, boldly amassed their forces to take the city. Babieca understood what was required of him and led El Cid's knights on a thundering charge that scattered their enemies in a blind terror, believing him risen from the dead. Valencia was saved

Eventually, Spain was fully reclaimed from the invaders. El Cid's tomb is located in the Burgos Cathedral, and Babieca's tomb is in the monastery of San Pedro de Cardeña. Babieca outlived his master by two years and was never mounted again following his legendary charge into the Moorish army bearing his dead master. He remarkably lived until the age of 40. El Cid and Babieca are immortalized in several impressive bronze statues, in both Spain and the U.S. and in a blockbuster movie with Charlton Heston. *(above left) (cited from: http://andalusianworld.com/site/the-legend-of-el-cid-and-babieca-andalusians-in-history-and-mythology/)*

Bucephalus

Bucephalus was Alexander the Great's horse and is considered by some to be the most famous horse in history. Alexander and Bucephalus' initial meeting was unique but demonstrated the true character of one of the greatest generals in all of history. Initially, Bucephalus was brought to Macedonia and presented to King Phillip II (Alexander's father) in 346 BCE by Philoneicus of Thessaly. With a price tag almost 3 times the norm (13 talents), the beautiful black horse stood taller than the normal Macedonian steed but was considered too wild and unmanageable, rearing up against anyone who came near him. Phillip ordered him led away.

Alexander sat in the audience with his mother Olympias watching the spectacle before him. As the attendants tried to lead Bucephalus away, Alexander rose calling them spineless. According to Plutarch's biography of Alexander, the young prince said, "What an excellent horse do they lose for want of address and boldness to manage him." At first Phillip ignored the challenge, but finally said to Alexander, "Do you reproach those who are older than yourself, as if you were better able to manage him than they?" Alexander, ignoring his father's remark, repeated his challenge and said he would pay for the horse if he, Alexander, were unable to tame him.

Amid wild laughter, Alexander approached the horse, he would name Bucephalus, calmly. He had realized something the others had not --- the horse was afraid of his own shadow. Turning Bucephalus toward the sun, so his shadow was behind him and slowly taking the reins in his hand, Alexander mounted him. The laughter of the crowd turned to cheers as Alexander rode off.

According to Plutarch, as Alexander returned to the arena with Bucephalus and dismounted, Phillip said, "O my son look thee out a kingdom equal to and worthy of thyself, for Macedonia is too little for thee." Historians claim this taming of the wild Bucephalus was a turning point in the young prince's life, demonstrating the confidence and determination he was to show in his conquest of Asia.

Bucephalus and Alexander were inseparable; only Alexander could ride him, and indeed he did, into every battle from the conquest of the Greek city-states and Thebes through Gaugamela and into India. After the final defeat of Darius, Bucephalus was kidnapped while Alexander was away on an excursion. Upon returning and learning of the theft, Alexander promised to fell every tree, lay the countryside to waste, and slaughter every inhabitant in the region. The horse was soon returned along with a plea for mercy.

Although historians disagree on the cause of the horse's death - some claim he died from battle wounds - most agree he died of old age after the Battle of Hydaspes River (326 BCE). While Plutarch spoke of both possible causes of death, he cites Onesicritus, a historian who accompanied Alexander on his conquests, as stating the horse died of old age. However, Bucephalus died, in mourning, Alexander founded a city in his beloved horse's memory and named it Bucephala. It is also interesting that Alexander built and named another city after his favorite dog Peritas. *(cited from: https://www.ancient.eu/Bucephalus/)*

Marengo

Marengo carried Napoleon in the Battle of Austerlitz, Battle of Jena-Auerstedt, Battle of Wagram, and Battle of Waterloo. He also was frequently used in the 80-mile gallops from Valladolid to Burgos, which he often completed in five hours.

As one of fifty-two horses in Napoleon's stud, Marengo fled with the rest of the High Command when it was overrun and the stables raided by the victorious Russian troops in their counter-offensive in 1812. The horse survived the retreat from Moscow and remained with the French High Command right up until the stallion was captured in 1815 at the Battle of Waterloo by English forces commanded by William Henry Francis Petre.

Napoleon was not a skilled rider. His father was not wealthy, and the family did not own a horse, so Napoleon did not grow up knowing how to ride. As Napoleon gained a reputation for displaying courage and clever tactics, he was soon given command of a French artillery force, and so, of course, he required some horses on which to inspect his troops on the battlefield. Napoleon preferred lightly boned Arabs or Barbs over the more popular Thoroughbreds used by most other military leaders. He liked the smaller horses because he could mount them without help, and the ones he chose to ride had been trained to perfection. But once he was in the saddle, his poor horsemanship was glaringly obvious; he grabbed the reins and bunched them in one hand, his toes pointed south, he slouched over and moved so much in the saddle that he wore holes in his breeches. However, while his posture and position might have elicited giggles from onlookers, he was absolutely fearless galloping his horses over any terrain, getting back up and on after numerous falls, and riding up to 50 miles a day if needed. He also preferred stallions.

Napoleon Bonaparte re-opened many of the stud farms that had been closed during the revolution. He created thirty stallion centers, three riding schools and encouraged the sport of horse racing as he hoped that bloodlines would improve as breeders competed to create faster horses. He also had an enlightened attitude towards some age-old customs such as docking tails. He would not allow horses with docked tails to be bought for himself or for the cavalry as he realized that horses get irritated and annoyed when they cannot swish flies away with short tails.

Napoleon kept a stable of eighty horses that he used for his personal use along with carriage horses but over his lifetime records show that he probably owned and used over one hundred fifty horses. Marengo, 1793–1831, was Napoleon' favorite war horse and was imported from Egypt as a six-year-old in 1799 after the Battle of Aboukir. It is believed that he was bred at the well-known El Naseri Stud. He would prove to be reliable and incredibly tough despite being just 14.1 h.h. and would often take part in eighty-mile gallops in around five hours.

Marengo was wounded eight times before being captured in 1815 during the Battle of Waterloo. William Henry Francis Petre, 11th Baron, brought him back to England and the horse was considered a real prize when sold to Lieutenant-Colonel Angerstein of the Grenadier Guards. Marengo stood at stud at the age of twenty-seven, but was not successful as a stallion and didn't sire any notable racehorses or even any winners. The horse died at thirty-eight years of age, an incredibly long life considering what he had lived through.

During his life in England, Marengo was a star attraction at public events. Marengo was displayed at exhibitions in Pall Mall and was shown alongside Napoleon's saddle, bridle, and boots. His battle scars along with the bullet that stayed in his tail were mentioned along with the Imperial crown and letter N that were branded on his hindquarters.

Today, parts of Marengo are still on display. After the Changing of the Guard Ceremony at Buckingham Palace in London, when the Captain sits down to lunch, in front of him, he will see one of Marengo's hooves covered with a polished silver lid. When the item (a snuff box) is not in use on the table, it sits on the nearby sideboard. On the lid is the inscription that reads, Hoof of Marengo, Barb charger of Napoleon, ridden by him at Marengo, Austerlitz, Jena, Wagram, in the campaign of Russia and lastly at Waterloo. This hoof was presented on April 8, 1840, by J.W. Angerstein Captain Grenadier Guards and Lieutenant-Colonel to his brother officers of the Household Brigade. Marengo's other two hooves are on display with his preserved skeleton at the Waterloo Gallery at the National Army Museum in Chelsea. *(cited from: https://horse-canada.com/horses-and-history/marengo-napoleons-favourite-horse/)*

Incitatus

The Roman emperor Caligula is best known today for his decadent, brutal and scandalous reign. One of his most trusted advisors was a horse!

According to Suetonius, an ancient historian, Caligula's horse Incitatus had a stable made of marble and a stall made of ivory. He wore only purple blankets, the color of royalty, and had jewels hanging from around his neck. The horse had its own servants, and its oats were mixed with gold flakes. The emperor would issue invitations on the horse's behalf inviting dignitaries to dinners attended by the horse's servants and would host lavish birthday parties in the horse's honor.

The emperor planned on making the horse an official member of the Roman government. According to historian Aloys Winterling, author of "Caligula: A Biography" (2011), insanity isn't the only logical explanation for such behavior. In his book, Winterling makes the case that many of the emperor's wackier stunts, including his treatment of Incitatus, were designed to insult and humiliate senators and other elites. By bestowing a high public office on his horse, then, Caligula aimed to show his underlings that their work was so meaningless an animal could do it. *(cited from: http://www.hitsshows.com/hits-blog/3-horses-that-changed-history)*

Figure

While many people have likely heard of the Morgan horse breed — one of the earliest breeds developed in the United States — far fewer know about the much-loved horse who started the lineage, Figure.

Figure was a small bay stallion, who stood just 14 hands high. But despite his smallish size, he was strong, fast and had a stylish way of moving. At three years old, he was given to Justin Morgan, a music teacher, and composer, as payment for a debt Morgan was owed. While under Morgan's care, Figure gained fame for his abilities as a workhorse and his speed as a racehorse. Figure famously beat two New York racehorses in a 1796 sweepstakes race, and he became known as the Justin Morgan horse.

According to the American Morgan Horse Association, "Figure's ability to out-walk, out-trot, outrun, and out-pull other horses were legendary. His stud services were offered throughout the Connecticut River Valley and various Vermont locations over his lifetime. However, his most valuable asset was the ability to pass on his distinguishing characteristics, not only to his offspring but through several generations."

The features and talents that made Figure stand out could still be readily spotted in his get. He continued to sire foals even as he was traded from owner to owner in his later years and he was used for everything from logging to racing to being a parade mount. In 1819, he was sold to his final owner, Levi Bean. He was put out to pasture and in 1821 died after being injured by a kick from another horse.

The legendary sire of a new breed of horse is at the center of author Marguerite Henry's "Justin Morgan Had a Horse" as well as a 1972 film by Walt Disney Studios with the same name. All Morgan horses today can trace back to this one horse! *(cited from: https://www.mnn.com/earth-matters/animals/photos/10-famous-horses-from-history/equine-celebrities-throughout-centuries#top-desktop)*

picture above – statute of Figure at the UVM Morgan Horse Farm

Copenhagen

Many of the most famous equines in history are those that served alongside humans during war. This is true for a 15-hand-high, ornery stallion named Copenhagen who gained fame after carrying the Duke of Wellington for seventeen consecutive hours in the Battle of Waterloo.

Copenhagen was born in 1808 and was of thoroughbred and Arabian stock. The latter breed likely gave him particular stamina and his fiery temperament.

When the Duke dismounted Copenhagen after the lengthy battle, he gave Copenhagen a pat of gratitude on the flank. But his grumpy — and apparently tireless — steed nearly took his head off with a sharp kick. According to The Regency Redingote: "Copenhagen very nearly achieved what the French had failed to do throughout that grueling battle. But the Duke was quick enough to avoid that lethal hoof, the last danger he would face on that terrible day. His groom took the stallion's reins and led him away for a well-deserved rub-down and rest. Years later, and after a long retirement, Copenhagen died at the age of twenty-eight." *(cited from: https://www.mnn.com/earth-matters/animals/photos/10-famous-horses-from-history/equine-celebrities-throughout-centuries#top-desktop)*

61

Comanche

Comanche is often cited as the only survivor of the Battle of Little Big Horn. Technically, roughly 100 other horses survived but were captured by the victors. He was thought to be part Mustang, part Morgan. The mount of Captain Myles Keogh, Comanche was seriously wounded in the battle, including seven bullet wounds. Members of the Army found him in a ravine two days later. He was collected and cared for, and he soon recovered from his wounds.

This wasn't the first time the stoic horse had to tough out injuries. Indeed, his toughness is what earned him his name. During a battle against the Comanche in 1868, he was shot by an arrow in the rump and yet continued on with Keogh on his back. After that day, he was named "Comanche" as a way to honor his bravery and steadfastness. He was wounded some twelve times during battles, including those injuries sustained during his final battle at Little Big Horn.

After Comanche was retired in 1878, Colonel Samuel D. Sturgis issued an order stating that the horse, "being the only living representative of the bloody tragedy of the Little Big Horn, June 25th, 1876, his kind treatment and comfort shall be a matter of special pride and solicitude on the part of every member of the Seventh Cavalry to the end that his life be preserved to the utmost limit." The order included that Comanche would have a comfortable stable, that he'd never be ridden again or have to work under any circumstances. Comanche was allowed to wander the parade grounds at his leisure, became a favorite pet of the soldiers at Fort Riley, and apparently enjoyed his fair share of beer. Not a bad retirement for a war horse.

When he died at the age of about twenty-nine in 1891, he was given a military funeral with full military honors, one of only two horses in the United States to be honored in such a way. His remains were preserved, and he can be seen on display at the University of Kansas Natural History Museum. *(cited from: https://www.mnn.com/earth-matters/animals/photos/10-famous-horses-from-history/equine-celebrities-throughout-centuries#top-desktop)*

Sargent Reckless

Sargent Reckless is perhaps the most decorated horse in U.S. military history. The young mare became part of the U.S. Marine Corps in 1952 when Lieutenant Eric Pedersen purchased the mare for $250 from a Korean stable boy at the Seoul racetrack who needed money to buy an artificial leg for his sister. The mare became a pack horse carrying ammunition for recoilless — or "reckless" — rifles and other supplies to the soldiers during the Korean War.

According to Robin Hutton, "During a five-day battle, on one day alone she made fifty-one trips from the Ammunition Supply Point to the firing sites, 95% of the time by herself. She carried three hundred eighty-six rounds of ammunition (over 9,000 pounds — almost 5 TONS! — of ammunition), walked over thirty-five miles through open rice paddies and up steep mountains with enemy fire coming in at the rate of five hundred rounds per minute. As she so often did, she would carry wounded soldiers down the mountain to safety, unload them, get reloaded with ammo, and off she would go back up to the guns."

As beloved as she was for her bravery, she was also famous for her appetite. The Marine Corp Association and Foundation notes that she, "liked to supplement her diet with what the Marines were eating. She once strolled near the galley tent and ate some scrambled eggs that were offered to her. She then washed them down with coffee. On later occasions, Reckless ate bacon and buttered toast with her scrambled eggs." Despite her diet and the many bullets whizzing around her, the horse survived the war and was recognized for her role. Reckless was brought back to the United States in 1954 where she was cared for by the 5th Marines. She was promoted to staff sergeant in 1959 then retired with full military honors in 1960. The mare was the recipient of two Purple Hearts, Good Conduct Medal, Presidential Unit Citation with star, National Defense Service Medal, Korean Service Medal, United Nations Service Medal and Republic of Korea Presidential Unit Citation. Several books have been written about this remarkable and quirky little horse. She gave birth to four foals in America and died in May 1968. A plaque and photo were dedicated in her honor at the Marine Corps Base Camp Pendleton stables and a statue of her was dedicated on July 26, 2013, at the National Museum of the Marine Corps in Quantico, Virginia. On May 12, 2018, a bronze statue of Sergeant Reckless was placed and dedicated in the Kentucky Horse Park, Lexington Kentucky. *(cited rom: https://www.mnn.com/earth-matters/animals/photos/10-famous-horses-from-history/equine-celebrities-throughout-centuries#top-desktop and https://en.wikipedia.org/wiki/Sergeant_Reckless)*

Beautiful Jim Key

This handsome horse was a performer during the turn of the 20th century. He was known as the smartest horse on earth and could, among many skills, count and do math, spell words by selecting letters from an alphabet, cite bible verses, tell time, use a phone, and take cash to a cash register and bring back correct change.

The horse and his trainer were a huge act, traveling around the country performing before amazed audiences from 1897 to 1906. They were the biggest act of the 1904 St. Louis World's Fair. By the end of their tours, they were seen by an estimated ten million people.

But perhaps equally as wonderful as the horse's abilities was the story of his trainer. "Dr." William Key was a former slave and a self-taught veterinarian who advocated for the kind treatment of animals. He trained Beautiful Jim without the use of a whip.

Anita Lequoia writes, "Animal organizations took note of the excellent treatment Beautiful Jim received, and activists that might normally picket animal acts instead presented Dr. Key and Jim with awards! William Key was the first African American recipient of MSPCA's Humanitarian Gold Medal, and Beautiful Jim Key was the first non-human recipient of multiple humane and literacy awards. Two million children joined the 'Jim Key Band of Mercy' and signed his pledge. The pledge simply stated, 'I promise to be kind to animals.' That's a mighty fine pledge!" Together, Doc Key and Beautiful Jim made strides toward the humane treatment of animals, and breaking down barriers for African Americans. *(cited rom: https://www.mnn.com/earth-matters/animals/photos/10-famous-horses-from-history/equine-celebrities-throughout-centuries#top-desktop)*

Trigger

Many horses gained fame in movies and television. One of the most famous was Trigger. Trigger was the palomino stallion and sidekick of Roy Rogers.

Born in 1932, Trigger was originally named Golden Cloud until he was tested out by Rogers as his potential mount for a film. Smiley Burnette, who played Roy's sidekick in his first two films, was watching and mentioned how quick on the trigger this horse was. Roy agreed and decided that Trigger was the perfect name for the horse. Roy purchased the horse for $2,500 and eventually outfitted him with a $5,000 gold and silver saddle.

It was a match made in heaven, as horse and cowboy worked wonderfully together. Over a period of almost twenty years, the original Trigger appeared in each of Roy's eighty-one starring films at Republic and all one hundred of Roy's television episodes. Trigger lived to the ripe old age of thirty-three. When he died, he was mounted and was on display in the Roy Rogers-Dale Evans Museum in Missouri until 2009. In 2010, he was sold at auction to cable network RFD-TV for $266,000.

(cited rom: https://www.mnn.com/earth-matters/animals/photos/10-famous-horses-from-history/equine-celebrities-throughout-centuries#top-desktop)

Chetak

Legend has it that a man who was a Charan by caste brought two young stallions as a gift to the then Maharana of Chittor, Udai Singh, father of Pratap. Pratap was just a young child then. The king asked the Charan what was so special about these horses. The Charan said that the father of these two horses was extremely powerful and could go miles before tiring and was a very intelligent war horse. The mother of these two horses was an exceptional mare of extraordinary strength. The names of the young fouls were Ketak and Chetak. Ketak was completely black, and Chetak was completely white in color. The Maharana then asked the Charan to demonstrate their strength. Ketak was chosen for experiment. Ketak was buried in the ground to his knees then was tapped to run. The horse was so powerful that it sprung into the air at once and started running with lightning speed. Nobody had expected this. Soon the men on their horses started chasing him. The horse kept running miles and miles and many chasing horses were soon breathless.

Ketak was young, wild, immature and untrained. After running fiercely for fifty miles, he died. When everything calmed down people noticed that there were hoofs of Ketak where he was kept. When it sprung into the air, it lost all of its hoofs and started running without them and eventually died due to bleeding. Everyone was shocked and sad. The Maharana then asked the Charan what he could do for him in return. The Charan asked for guardianship of his son at the royal house. This wish was granted. Maharana kept Chetak and gave it to young Pratap.

Chetak belonged to the Marwari breed. He was small in size measuring somewhere between 14.2 to 15.2 hands height. He had a slender body as that of a desert bred horse. Its high forehead was highly expressive combined with a long face and brilliantly sparkling eyes.

 On June 21, 1576, a smaller Rajput army lead by Rana Pratap fought the Mughal army at Haldighati for the independence of Mewar. Three interesting things can be seen in the statue commemorating the event *(left above)*. Rana's horse Chetak has an artificial trunk attached to his face. The Rajput army had disguised their cavalry with artificial trunks so that the Mughal elephants would confuse them with their own elephants and would not attack them. As Rana Pratap charged with his bhala (javelin), Man Singh ducks behind his mahawat (driver). The driver was killed by the javelin while Man Singh survived. Man Singh's elephant has a sword attached to its trunk. As Pratap's horse moved away after the attack, the elephant cut off one of its hind legs. As the Mughals surrounded Pratap, the brave horse, Chetak, carried off his master away from the battlefield on his three working legs. On reaching safe grounds, Chetak died. *(cited from: https://www.quora.com/What-is-the-story-of-Chetak-the-horse-of-King-Maharana-Pratap and http://india-historyofournation.blogspot.com/2013/11/images-from-indian-history-rana-pratap.html)*

Horses in Art

The beauty and nobility of the horse has been captured in works of art for 30,000 years. From cave art to impressive sculptures and stunning paintings the horse has been romanticized and idealized by humans in countless artistic forms.

Da Vinci's Horse

Leonardo's "Horse That Never Was" would have assured his unparalleled reputation as a sculptor. This is the romantic story of Leonardo's unfulfilled passion, the resurrection of the idea by Charles C. Dent.

During the seventeen years that followed the Duke of Sforza's 1482 commission of the largest equine statue ever conceived, Leonardo da Vinci also worked on one of his masterpiece paintings, The Last Supper, and a series of portraits of Italian nobles. He also produced a city plan for Milan, new weapons designs, and a defense system for the castle that the Duke probably should have taken more seriously. The Duke also expected Leonardo to create stage sets, manage gala parties and compose rhymes and puzzles for the ladies of the Court. Royal sponsorship clearly did not always release Leonardo to pursue his artistic endeavors.

A 24-foot clay model would finally dominate the landscape in a vineyard near the Duke's castle. The Horse was to be cast in bronze according to a revolutionary method that was detailed in Leonardo's carefully-created notebooks. Scholar Carlo Pedretti describes this place, "That site, which is today a dense and noisy urban district, was then a pleasant expanse of open fields, dotted with trees and shrubs, or neatly kept as orchards, vineyards or citrus groves. One can well imagine the skyline of such a peaceful landscape, bathed in the yellow light of a misty morning of a September day

in the Lombard plain … and see that skyline suddenly interrupted by the imposing silhouette of Leonardo's colossal clay model, standing there with the foreboding of a Trojan horse." That must have been the way the Gascon bowmen of the French troops saw it when they entered Milan on Sept. 10, 1499. Instead of admiring the model's majesty, however, the victorious French archers used it for target practice, reducing it tragically to a mound of clay.

Leonardo would not attempt the project again and died on May 2, 1519. Legend has it that he never ceased mourning his lost horse. Many of the working sketches for The Horse were lost over the centuries that followed. One set of notebooks, known as the Windsor Collection, came into the possession of the British royal family. Another collection, now known as the Codex Madrid II, was discovered in Madrid's Biblioteca Nacional in 1966.

An article in the Sept. 1977 issue of National Geographic magazine about Leonardo would launch a new existence not only for Leonardo's horse, but also for Charles C. Dent, a retired airline pilot, artist and art collector living in Fogelsville, Pennsylvania. The romantic legend, with its combination of creative genius and human frailty, cast its spell over Dent. Charlie Dent decided that Leonardo and Italy should have The Horse. To formalize The Horse project, Charles C. Dent formed Leonardo da Vinci's Horse, Inc. (LDVHI) officially in 1982. He took up the horse's reins and remained at full gallop for the rest of his life. Sculptor Nina Akamu was hired in 1997 to complete The Horse after the death of Charles C. Dent. He studied Leonardo's entire body of work along with his sketches of The Horse to interpret the design correctly. The project was championed by Fred Meijer in the late 1990's, resulting in two casts of the 24-foot monument—one for Meijer Gardens in Grand Rapids, Michigan *(above)* and one for the city of Milan, Italy. *(cited from: http://www.davincisciencecenter.org/about/leonardo-and-the-horse/the-full-story-of-leonardos-horse/)*

George Stubbs

George Stubbs (1724-1806) was an English painter. Classified in his lifetime as a sporting painter, as such he was excluded from full membership of the Royal Academy. He is best remembered for his paintings of horses. Having studied anatomy, Stubbs's paintings of horses are among the most accurate ever painted.

Frederic Remington

Frederic Remington (1861-1909) was an American painter, illustrator, sculptor, and writer who specialized in depictions of the Old American West, specifically concentrating on images of cowboys, American Indians, and the U.S. Cavalry.

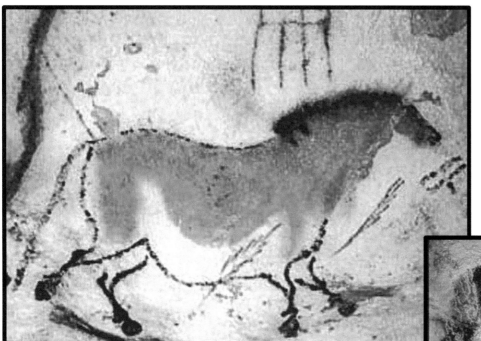

Cave Art

Lascaux is the setting of a complex of caves in southwestern France. Over 600 wall paintings cover the interior walls and ceilings of the cave. The age of the paintings is estimated at around 17,000 years. *(left)*

Chauvet-Pont-d'Arc Cave paintings in southern France *(right)* were discovered in 1994 and are believed to have been created 33,500 to 37,000 years ago.

Currier and Ives

Currier and Ives was a successful American printmaking firm based in New York City from 1835 to 1907. The prolific firm produced prints from paintings by fine artists as black and white lithographs that were hand colored. Small works sold for five to twenty cents each, and large works sold for $1 to $3 each.

Portraits

Portraits of people riding a horse have always been associated with status with the implication that a noble warrior or ruler or person of high status was being depicted.

George III with the Prince of Wales by Beechey (1798)

Charles I by Van Dyck (1637)

Phillip III by Diego Velázquez (1634)

George Washington
by Rembrandt Peale (1808)

The Medici Family - Procession of the Youngest
King

Queen Victoria
by Francis Grant (1840)

You and Your "Unicorn"

In the process of reading these myths and legends and real-life stories, have you decided that, if you don't already own a horse, you may NEED a horse? In the next few pages, there are some helpful tips for finding your very own "unicorn."

Finding a Horse of Your Own

The Horse

Where in this wide world can man find nobility without pride,
friendship without envy, or beauty without vanity?
Here where grace is laced with muscle and strength by gentleness confined.

———

He serves without servility; he has fought without enmity.
There is nothing so powerful, nothing less violent;
there is nothing so quick, nothing more patient.

———

England's past has been borne on his back.
All our history is in his industry.
We are his heirs;
He is our inheritance.

Ronald Duncan

Get Educated!

Contact the association(s) of the breeds that interest you.
Most breed associations have web sites. Contact them! They are usually happy to promote their breed by sending you information or helping you find events and horses in your area.

Read horse magazines
There are so many magazines available to help to educate you. Some are focused on disciplines like dressage magazines or driving magazines or trail riding. Some are focused on breeds of horses. Some concentrate on general horse care. There are magazines for almost every aspect of horse ownership. American Horse Publications is a good place to start to find publications.
https://www.americanhorsepubs.org/

Visit horse farms
Find horse farms in your area that have open houses or call to arrange a visit. It is always best to call first; many are private farms that are not open to the public but may welcome a visit from a potential new horse owner. There are breeding farms and training farms and pleasure farms. It's best to look at as many a possible to help you get an idea of what kind of horse you may want and what disciplines interest you.

Go to horse shows

Going to horse shows is also a way to discover the many events available for horse owners in your area. Breed associations, 4-H clubs and training barns are good places to start to find events in your area.

Go to horse expos

Many states have large expos once a year. These expos will have vendors and speakers and demonstrations. Attending an Expo is a great "one stop shopping" opportunity.

Examine Your Resources

Time

Will you be taking care of your horse at home or boarding your horse? If you ae going to keep the horse at home, do you know how to care for a horse and do you have the time to do that? Horses need care 365 days a year! If you are going to board the horse, how often will you be able to be with the horse?

Money

Buying the horse is just the beginning! Be sure you understand all of the other costs involved – feed, hay, farrier, vet, farm equipment and tack are just a few of the basics. When you visit farms, look around and become aware of all of the things involved in horse ownership.

Skills

Sometimes it is best to take lessons first before buying a horse. This will help you to decide on the type of horse you want and the discipline you may want to pursue. Working as a groom or doing barn chores will help you to decide if this is really something you want to do and the skills you learn will come in handy if and when you do buy a horse.

Selecting the Right Horse

Temperament
It's important to match the temperament of the horse to that of the owner. Be sure to visit the horse several times before deciding. Just like people, horses have good days and bad days. Enlist the aid of a professional when you go to look at horses. Their experience will help to determine if the horse is a good match for you.

Size
Pony vs. horse - small horse vs. large horse. Small does not mean easier and big does not mean more difficult. Just like the color of the horse, size often does not matter. There are other things that are much more important. Children do not NEED to start on a pony; there are plenty of lovely horses well suited to children

Age
Young or green horses are not always best for first time owners, but older horses may come with bad habits. Again, getting the assistance of a professional who can ride the horse to try it out and knows your abilities is always a good idea. If the horse does need more training, can you afford that? Good training takes a long time and can be rewarding with the right help.

Gender

It's true that geldings, as opposed to mares, are usually the same 365 days a year but many people do prefer mares for various reasons. The gender of your horse really is a personal preference. Bottom line is, you need to get along with the horse's temperament. If a horse does not live up to its potential for you, that does not mean, "oh well, I can use it for breeding." Only the best stock should be used to breed; leave breeding to the breeders!

Suitability for a Discipline

Do you want to cut cows with your horse or do you want to jump your horse or drive your horse? Chances are the same horse will not do each discipline equally well. You may want to decide what you want to do and find a horse suited for that discipline. That does not mean you can't do several different disciplines with your horse; it's just more likely that the horse will excel at only 1 or maybe 2 disciplines. Some breeds are known for their versatility. If you want to do several different disciplines, choose a breed that is known to be versatile but again, that horse will most likely not excel at every discipline you try – but you will have fun!

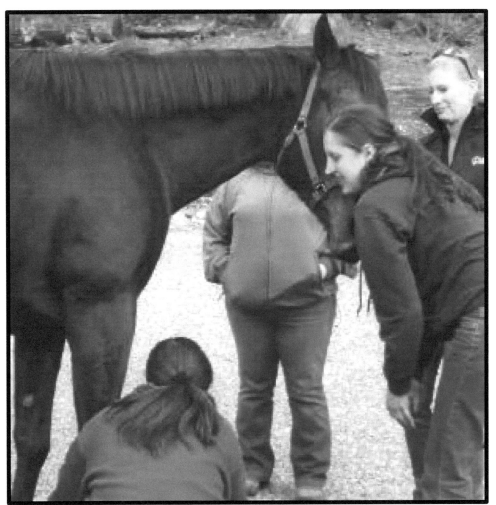

Communicate with the Seller

Pictures and Videos

The internet certainly makes finding horses much easier. Pictures and videos can help a buyer to narrow down the hunt for a horse. But remember, pictures and videos are only a moment in time; you need to actually see the horse in person to help make a good decision.

Ask Questions

Caveat Emptor - it's the buyer's responsibility to ask the questions. No question is a dumb one! Be sure to be honest with the seller about your abilities, expectations, plans and finances. Only look at what you can afford and be sure to keep in mind the cost of any additional training the horse may need.

Records

Be sure to ask for detailed records. Most owners will have health records that include deworming, vaccinations, x-rays and more. Training records are important to ask about too. Who trained the horse? When? For What? For how long? You can also ask for show records. But don't make the mistake of buying a horse because he/she is a "winning" horse. Not all wins are equal. Sometimes a horse will become a winner with a new owner but never won with the current owner and the opposite can be true too. Most importantly, keep in mind that winning isn't everything!

Horse Habits

Be sure to ask if the horse has any stable vices like cribbing or weaving; some vices never show up while you are looking at the horse so you need to ask. Ask questions about daily handling of the horse. If you can't do 24-hour turnout and that is what the horse is used to, it could change the horse's behavior. Ask if the horse is compatible with other horses…after all, horses are like potato chips and some times you can't have just one so your herd may grow!

Riding

When you go to try the horse be part of getting the horse ready; this is an important part of really seeing the nature of the horse. Ask questions about the horse's habits and general disposition as you are getting the horse ready. Have the owner ride the horse first and, if you brought a trainer, be sure that he/she also rides the horse; they should know what will be a good match for you and, knowing your abilities, can coach you when you try the horse.

85

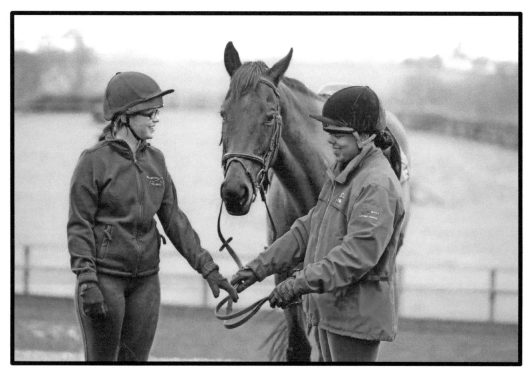

The Purchase Process

Warranties

You've found the horse of your dreams and now it's time to welcome the horse to your family. The seller may wish to state something about vices or restricted use for which the horse is being sold. Check with an attorney if you are unsure about signing this.

Documentation

Sellers usually have contracts so be sure to read it carefully. Some breeds of horses have registration papers. If the horse has papers ask who will handle and pay for the transfer. If the horse does not have papers, find out why and be sure it is eligible to be registered.

Trial Periods and Leases

Your trainer may suggest a trial period. Terms for a trial period must be spelled out in writing to protect both the buyer and seller. Some sellers will also be willing to lease the horse. Make sure all of the particulars about the care of the horse, what you are allowed to do with the horse, training etc. are well spelled out in the lease agreement.

Pre-purchase Exam

The veterinarian who does the exam is usually not the horse's vet due to conflict of interest so you will have to arrange for a vet to do the exam.

The exam will give you an idea of the horse's current health and an outlook for what the future will bring. A basic exam will check eyes, heart, lungs, teeth, basic soundness and x-rays if needed. The exam will help to determine if the horse will be able to do what you need and, if there are small issues, does everything else outweigh those issues.

After the Purchase

Life insurance and health insurance are available for horses and may be something you want to consider. Keep in touch with the seller; they like hearing about the horse and can also answer questions that may come up.

Now that you have a horse it's just the beginning of a wonderful relationship. You will soon find out that you and your horse will never finished learning together. Horses provide opportunities to meet people and travel to new places. They teach us perseverance, patience, humility and unconditional love